IDITAROD DREAMS

IDITAROD DREAMS

**A year in the life of
Alaskan sled dog racer
DeeDee Jonrowe**

Lew Freedman & DeeDee Jonrowe

Epicenter Press

Fairbanks/Seattle

Editor: Christine Ummel
Cover design: Leslie Newman
Cover photos: Jeff Schultz, Alaska Stock Images © 1994
Map: Ed Walker/Leslie Newman
Inside design and typesetting: Newman Design/Illustration
Photos: Jeff Schultz, Alaska Stock Images; Lew Freedman;
collection of DeeDee Jonrowe; Roy Corral
Printer: Best Book Manufacturing

Library of Congress Cataloging-in-Publication Data

Freedman, Lewis.
    Iditarod dreams : a year in the life of Alaskan sled dog racer DeeDee
Jonrowe / by Lew Freedman and DeeDee Jonrowe.
        p.   cm.
    ISBN 0-945397-29-1
    1. Jonrowe, DeeDee, 1953– . 2. Sled dog racing—Alaska. 3. Iditarod
Trail Sled Dog Race, Alaska. 4. Mushers—Alaska—Biography. 5. Women
mushers—Alaska—Biography. I. Jonrowe, DeeDee, 1953– . II. Title.
SF440.15.J67F74   1995
798´.8—dc20
[B]   94-42403
                                                                    CIP

To order single copies of IDITAROD DREAMS, mail $13.95 each (Washing-
ton state residents add $1.14 sales tax) plus $2 for book rate shipping to: Epicenter
Press, Box 82368, Kenmore Station, Seattle, WA 98028.

Booksellers: Retail discounts are available from our trade distributor, Graphic Arts
Center Publishing Co., Box 10306, Portland, OR 97210. Phone 800-452-3032.

First printing, January, 1995
10 9 8 7 6 5 4 3 2 1

PRINTED IN CANADA

To all the mushers and dogs who
brave the obstacles of the Iditarod Trail

Other books by Lew Freedman...

*Dangerous Steps: Vernon Tejas and the Solo
Winter Ascent of Mount McKinley*

Real Alaskans

*Live from the Kenai River: Reelin' 'Em in
with Celebrity Fishing Guide Harry Gaines*

*Iditarod Classics: Tales of the Trail Told by the
Men and Women Who Race Across Alaska*

George Attla: The Legend of the Sled Dog Trail

Live from the Tundra! Lew Freedman's Greatest Hits

Hunting the Wild Country (with Kenny Sailors)

TABLE OF CONTENTS

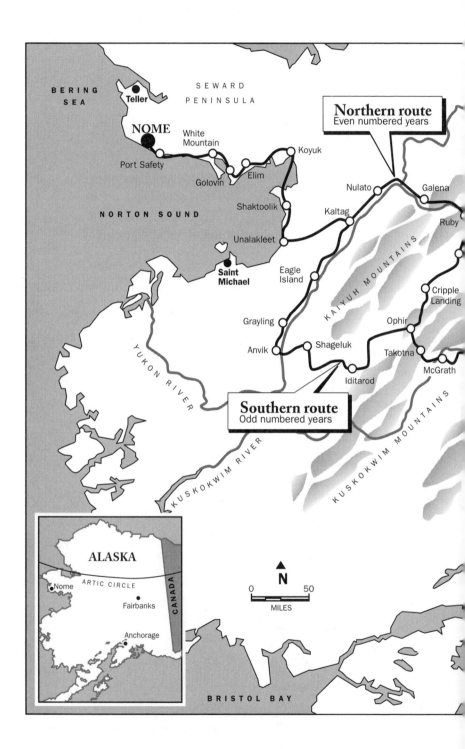

IDITAROD TRAIL SLED DOG RACE

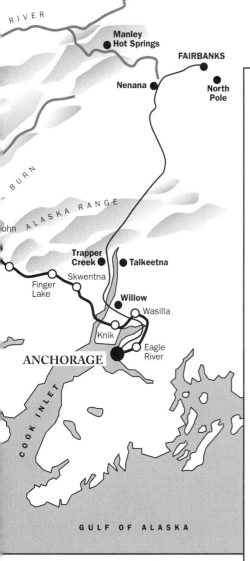

INTRODUCTION

Having covered the Iditarod Trail Sled Dog Race for more than a decade, I can enthusiastically state that this race, while not nearly as well-known or publicized as the Super Bowl, the Kentucky Derby, or the Indianapolis 500, is one of the great sporting events in the nation.

The Iditarod is an endurance event typically lasting ten or eleven days, and it is accompanied by the wildest and craziest of variables — winter weather in Alaska. No indoor stadiums for this sport. No nice, neat 2 p.m. starting time, either. In fact, little is neatly packaged about the Iditarod. When the whims of the competitive conditions are determined by higher powers than mankind, or even the National Football League, you have to roll with the punches.

The Iditarod is always full of surprises. I remember going to bed one night late in the 1991 race absolutely certain that Susan Butcher would be crossing the finish line to claim her fifth title by noon the next day. I had forgotten the caveat "weather permitting." It turned out that we didn't get any finisher at all for two days because of the unbelievable storm that roared in. And the winner turned out to be Rick Swenson, claiming his unprecedented fifth championship, not Butcher.

The moral of that story, of course, is that it's never over until it's over.

To succeed in the 1,100-mile mush across the harsh terrain of Alaska, facing down blizzards and frightening temperatures, a racer must combine stamina, good judgment, strategy, and know-how, as well as possess a distinct spirit of adventure. And that's just the human coach of the team of hard-working huskies.

There is no event which unifies Alaskans like the Iditarod, no event which captures the attention and interest of the whole state the way the Iditarod does. The race for governor is a distant second behind the race to Nome, if that.

Although the Iditarod itself — which begins on the first Saturday in March in Anchorage, Alaska's largest city, and concludes when the seventy or so mushers finally make it all the way across the state to Nome on the Bering Sea Coast — began in 1973, competitive mushing has a long history in Alaska.

In fact, history is one reason why the Iditarod is so exciting. It is a throw-back event, one that evokes an earlier time when men and women faced distinct hardships to survive in Arctic conditions. If late 20th century Americans have grown soft because life has been made easier by so many new electrical conveniences, it was not so eighty or more years ago, especially in the Far North.

The jet plane may connect modern-day Alaska with the rest of the country, but a person who came north for the gold rush and settled down certainly needed a hardy spirit. Those who lived in the wild back then traveled by dog sled instead of city bus. It was the most practical way to get around in a country with no roads and before the advent of the airplane.

The roots of Iditarod mushing date back to 1908, when the residents of Nome invented the All-Alaska Sweepstakes. In this 408-mile race, mushers took their dog teams north to Candle, then turned around and mushed home to Nome. Many men earned their reputations for toughness by conquering the rugged trail and intense winds and snowstorms in those races, and their fame endures yet in Alaska. John "Iron Man" Johnson, Scotty Allan, and Leonhard Seppala are still respected for their feats. Seppala earned even greater fame in 1925 by playing an integral role in the diphtheria serum run that brought life-saving medicine to Nome by dog team.

When Joe Redington, Sr., and others created the Iditarod in 1973, they cited the successful serum run as their inspiration. Iditarod officials have never forgotten or overlooked the Iditarod's glorious predecessors, and neither have the fans of this more modern replica of those rugged frontier days.

There's something unique about the wild spirit of this race across Alaska. Mushing along the quiet trail in the stillness of night is an experience mushers rhapsodize about. Sometimes the most beautiful, electrifying, and spellbinding northern lights crinkle in the sky, offering a silent symphony to travel by. Mushers still recall the pink and red shimmering night they spent along the Yukon River and on into Unalakleet during the 1989 race — a red sky at midnight. Even Redington, the founder of the Iditarod, said he'd never seen anything like it in his thousands upon thousands of miles of sled dog travel.

There are more tangible rewards to success in the Iditarod. The winner earns $50,000, becomes an instant hero, and retains lasting fame in the 49th state. Many mushers who have never won the event are as popular as the champions, with their own statewide followings.

Every March, the Iditarod owns Alaska. Fans are hungry for every shred of news and gossip from the trail. A frenzy of excitement grips the nearly 600,000 residents of the state. The musher is king — or queen, since mushing is one of the few sports where men and women compete on equal footing.

As popular as mushers are during the race, I was surprised at the way they often disappeared completely from public view between Iditarods. I wondered what mushers did in their eleven-month off-season. Today's athletes no longer play a sport in season, then take off until the next year's training camp. What did mushers do the rest of the year? How did they prepare for the big race? How did they plan?

I thought the best way to delve into this rarely explored world behind the scenes was to spend a year with a top Iditarod musher.

My choice was DeeDee Jonrowe of Willow, Alaska, a musher who first competed in the Iditarod in 1980. As the 1993 Iditarod began, Jonrowe had a string of five consecutive top-ten finishes to her credit. She was a perennial contender, perhaps on the cusp of becoming champion of the Iditarod.

Jonrowe and I first met in 1989. She had just won the John Beargrease Sled Dog Marathon in Minnesota in record time and that seemed to stamp her as a contender in the upcoming Iditarod that March. Jonrowe's dominating, record-setting victory in the shorter race seemed to indicate she was about to move into the top echelon of Iditarod racers.

That idea led me to write a feature story about Jonrowe's win, her background, and her prospects. We spent a pleasurable afternoon sitting at the table in the kitchen of her airy Willow home. What I discovered that day, and have had reinforced many times since, is that Jonrowe is good company. She is chatty, friendly, and generally open with her thoughts about her sport and her life in mushing.

A graduate of the University of Alaska Fairbanks, Jonrowe lived for many years in Bethel, in the Alaska Bush, where she first raced dogs. She is one of the finest female mushers in a still male-dominated sport, and she is an outspoken, thoughtful, Christian woman with a competitive streak.

This story covers a year in the life of DeeDee Jonrowe, from the start of the 1993 Iditarod to the conclusion of the 1994 Iditarod. During that year, Jonrowe and I met frequently at her home for interviews, spoke often on the phone, had a rendezvous in a hotel coffee shop, went king salmon fishing on a major Alaska river, talked at the starting line and finish line of the Iditarod, and, well, you get the idea.

Offered here is a glimpse of the training program, the preparation time, and the daily life of a leading Iditarod musher. You will follow Jonrowe over the hazards of the trail and through a surprisingly hectic off-season as she tries to pack twenty-eight hours of living into twenty-four-hour days. You may wonder if Jonrowe ever stops moving at top speed between dawn and dusk. As I can attest, she is a woman in perpetual motion.

As the story progresses, you will experience the drama and adventure of being on the Iditarod Trail at the front of the pack with the world's best long-distance mushers. And you'll share Jonrowe's thoughts, reactions, and comments as each race unfolds, and her reflections on how the events of the 1993 race affected her preparation for the 1994 race.

Two separate blocks of time — racing on the trail and life away from the trail — are brought together here to show what makes Jonrowe a top Iditarod musher.

— Lew Freedman

It takes a year of hard work to reach the starting line.

CHAPTER 1

THE STARTING LINE

It was 7 a.m., March 6, 1993. I lay awake in bed at my parents' house with the start of my eleventh Iditarod Trail Sled Dog Race a couple of hours away.

These were my last moments of comfort under warm blankets for perhaps the next eleven days. When you are in a race like the Iditarod, mushing 1,100 miles across the state of Alaska, you grab cat naps, little snatches of rest, when you can. Your dogs need rest, but every minute you are sleeping you might be falling further behind your competitors. You stay in your clothes. You sleep on the floor of cabins. You doze on the back of your sled, hoping you don't fall off if you hit a bump, or get hit in the head by a tree branch when you've got your eyes closed.

My mom and dad live in Anchorage, only a few miles from the starting line of the Iditarod. It is nice to be able to roll out of bed in a cozy place and be on Fourth Avenue in minutes. I live in Willow, Alaska, 75 miles to the north, and if I had to drive to town for the start I'd be setting the alarm for 3 a.m. Just what you need — to be short of sleep even before the race begins.

On this morning, my dog team — the best team I'd ever assembled — was already at the starting position downtown. My husband, Mike, and my handler, Knut Soyland, had loaded the dogs into our truck and hauled them there at 5:30 so I could get every possible minute of rest. It was the last time I would be pampered for quite a while.

It's often tough to fall asleep before the race. Luckily, this time I got almost nine hours of sleep. When I was younger, just getting started in sled dog racing, I was a basket case before events. I could barely sleep at all the night before the race. In the middle of the night, I was looking for my headlamp, looking for batteries, getting my sled runners fixed. It was last-minute panic time. It's tough for rookies to get any rest before the start. They're too busy worrying about what awaits them.

Experience makes a difference. Still, I'm normally so excited before the Iditarod I can barely contain myself. It is the World Series of mushing events, the biggest and best-known sled dog race in the world. Before the 1993 race, I had a record of five top-ten finishes in a row, and I considered myself a serious contender for the $50,000 first-place prize in the twenty-first Iditarod.

But leaving my parents' house and heading to the starting line, I did not have my normal level of excitement for this race. The trouble was my health. I was starting out with a bad left knee and a bad right hand, injuries that I was afraid would haunt me on the trail.

Earlier in the year, I had broken my hand by smacking it on the side of a tree. Recent surgery had left me with a metal pin in my hand. I didn't know if it would hold up. Would it take the pounding over the rough terrain in the Farewell Burn? Would it bother me when temperatures reached 40 degrees below zero? A friend suggested that I not punch anyone during the race. Good idea. My hand probably would break apart like a shattered window.

I arrived at the starting line wearing my trademark, a colorful snowsuit designed by Eddie Bauer, one of my sponsors. For the 1993 race, Eddie Bauer made me a purple outfit, with the vest and parka decorated with doggie faces. Each step I took rubbed the pant legs together, making a *swish, swish* sound. The suit was thick, but where I was going I needed all the protection I could get from the elements.

"I WAS STARTING OUT WITH A BAD LEFT KNEE AND A BAD RIGHT HAND, INJURIES THAT I WAS AFRAID WOULD HAUNT ME ON THE TRAIL."

I also had handy one new item of gear that was not color-coordinated — a white knee brace. I had injured my knee a few months earlier, while racing in the Alpirod in France. The dogs were negotiating a downhill ski slope in the French Alps. We jogged around a curve and made a 90-degree turn, and the team bolted down the hill. I was dragged part of the way, and the knee hyperextended, tearing the ligaments.

Now it was a tossup whether my ligaments would hold together better if I wore the brace against bare skin or on the outside of the snowsuit. I could see it chafing on the skin or slipping on the clothing. I ended up wearing the knee brace wrapped tightly on the outside of my long underwear, guessing that would provide the best support.

These are not the kind of thoughts you want to have at the start of a race. You are supposed to be fresh, optimistic, looking ahead to the great adventure. I was definitely more preoccupied than usual, and I felt weaker because of the iffy condition of my hand and knee.

Since I am only 5' 2", weighing 130 pounds, I needed to be at full strength.

Given the uncertainty of my own powers, I was also scared of the terrain. All the things that had happened in past Iditarods were running through my mind. Many people who have never seen rural Alaska picture the Iditarod as a smooth ride, the dogs trotting powerfully, the sled runners sliding quietly over a groomed trail. Parts of the Iditarod are like that, but there are also areas of bare ground and iced-up hills, which can be dangerous. These come up early in the race. In the first 200 miles of the race, between Skwentna and Finger Lake and Rainy Pass, I've probably broken seven sleds over the years.

Some driving record, huh? Accidents happen numerous ways. You hit trees, hit tussocks, bounce off rocks. Gravel bars rip off pieces of the sled. A lot of places are really hard on sleds. I had grilled my husband, Mike, over and over. "Are you sure my toboggan is tough?" Now I felt that, short of being hit by a truck, the sled could handle anything that was out there.

For the start of the Iditarod, thousands of people line the street to watch us set out for Nome. A lot of mushers hate the Anchorage start. They don't like crowds. They worry that their dogs get too excited and jumpy. It's important for the race, though, since this is the only time most of the spectators get a chance to see mushers live. The rest of the time fans can only watch reports on television or read about the race in the newspaper. Even if it's the only time, we're real, live human beings to them on the first Saturday in March.

I drew start position number twenty-five, so even though the first musher went out at 9 a.m., I wouldn't be leaving until 9:50. It was only eight o'clock as I walked through the soft, dirty snow that was spread on the side streets to my truck. People I didn't even know began yelling, "Good luck, DeeDee!"

I try to smile or wave to everybody. If fans care enough to

LEW FREEDMAN

Lacing up my boots, I knew we would face obstacles in the race ahead.

wish me well, I owe them that much. More fans crowded around and leaned over the fencing, eager to talk about the race and to take pictures.

"So this is your year?" asked one.

"I hope so," I said.

A little boy asked how long I train.

"Months and months and months," I told him.

Boy, if he only knew. I doubt many people understand that mushing at the Iditarod level is a year-round occupation. You can't just decide to jump in the race a week before it starts and expect to get anywhere. This is a race of preparation and experience.

"You don't want to be noticed this year, do you DeeDee?" another fan yelled.

I laughed. I have red hair and had tied it back with green ribbons. Combining that with my colorful snowsuit, I guess I was as bright as a box of crayons. I did want to be noticed, though not for my attire. I wanted to be noticed for becoming champion of the Iditarod.

Many of the well-wishers were strangers, but a lot of people close to me — friends like Linda and Ray Williams, Bob and Robin Chlupach, my mom, Peggy Stout, and Mike — helped me on race morning. My dad, Ken Stout, was not there. He was having heart trouble. In the weeks leading up to the race, my parents didn't want to tell me about it. They made it sound as if he was just mildly sick, but I figured he was being protected way too much for only having the flu. They didn't want me to worry about it because they didn't think it would do him or me any good.

My little group made sure I wasn't mushing off and leaving any essential gear behind. They all helped me put my twenty dogs in harness. I had Elroy and Gypsy in lead. These two dogs were new at it, because my old, trusted leader Johnnie, my greatest dog, was in retirement. With these newcomers in charge, I was uncertain not only about my own abilities at the back of the team, but also about the leaders in front of the team.

On race day, my mom is at least as nervous as I am. She said the first year I raced the Iditarod in 1980, she watched me mush away from the start and thought, "There goes my little girl."

Given how inexperienced I was that year, she had good reason to worry. And knowing that I had an injured hand and an injured knee, she had good reason to worry in 1993.

How could I tell her not to worry? I was worried. It is a long way from Anchorage to Nome. Anything can happen along the Iditarod Trail — and often does.

I thought again about what the young boy had asked me. How long did I train?

A year. That's precisely it. A year's worth of practice, a year's worth of hard work, of planning, of short races, of coaching, training, and teaching the huskies, all leading up to start day. It's 354 days of preparation for 11 days of the main event.

My team was moving fast as we passed through Dalzell Gorge.

CHAPTER 2

THE RACE IS ON

The Iditarod wouldn't be the Iditarod if there weren't some adventures out there.

The first 20-mile stretch of the race runs along the highway between Anchorage and Eagle River. It's a commuter road during the week, and on race day the trail is lined with spectators. Mostly, the only thing you can do here is not hurt yourself. Going out and trying to win the race to Eagle River is really nuts. There's no point. No one is going to get an advantage that will set them up for the rest of the race. Instead, you want the team to be quiet, stay calm, take it easy.

One of my top dogs, Barkley, was just too excited being around so many people. He wanted to leave the trail to grab cameramen or children's hats and gloves. This was good to know because later I would have to depend on Barkley as a leader. Now I knew I didn't want him running the show when we were in thick with spectators, even in a village. Throughout the rest of the race, I would have to stop him from grabbing for cameras and children's gloves.

The point of the Anchorage start and the run to Eagle River is to give as many people as possible in the most populous area of the state a chance to see us mushing. At Eagle River, we loaded our dogs into a truck and drove them 30 miles to Wasilla for the afternoon restart.

On the way I drove my truck off to a secluded area, parked, and fed the dogs. I gave them water and Formula One. It's a high-protein, high-caloric, top-of-the-line dog food with a meat base. A hard-working dog may burn 7,000 calories a day on the Iditarod Trail, so you bet it's got to be good stuff.

I ate a high-protein, high-caloric salmon salad sandwich. Though I don't think I burn 7,000 calories a day on the trail, sometimes it feels like 7 million.

The restart in Wasilla is at the small airport. They send us out off a runway, just like a jet. Wasilla is another big gathering place for fans. That makes it interesting. You've got twenty dogs raring to go — which is a lot of power — and you're trying to control them. All the teams are close together. It's hard to pass. My heart was beating fast. This is the true start. When we mush out of Wasilla, we are mushing into the wilderness.

Again, you're in a situation where there's little point in trying to win the race in the first hour. It's 11 miles later, in Knik Lake, where the racing begins in earnest. Until you reach Knik Lake, you're pulling two sturdy sleds, with a rider on the second one, for ballast. Mike rode in my second sled. Having Mike with me, whether it's in training or at the start and restart, is always an asset. I find that I'm always more emotionally driven when he's beside me, encouraging me.

At Knik Lake, you switch to a lightweight racing sled that carries all your mandatory gear. Husbands are not considered mandatory gear, so it was goodbye to Mike until the finish line.

Under Iditarod rules you must be prepared for an emergency in the wilderness. You are required to carry snowshoes, an axe, booties, dog food, a sleeping bag, and a cooker at all times. My sled and gear combined weighed about 120 pounds. You try to keep the total weight under 100, but that's really impossible.

After Knik Lake, you are on the trail to Nome. The crowds, the roads, are all behind you. By this time on the first day, it's also dark. It's different traveling at night than during the day. Sometimes it is terrifically beautiful, with a clear, dark sky and a million stars lighting the way. You need to have a headlamp, though, and when it's cloudy and overcast you're fearful it will blink off at the wrong time.

It was dark as I headed out on the Little Susitna River. I looked forward to reaching Flathorn Lake, where Sue Firmin lives. She's an old, close friend, and we spent long hours together on the trail when I first started in the Iditarod. In recent years, her knee has been operated on several times and hasn't allowed her to race. It was sobering to think that Sue had retired from racing because of a bad knee, and here I was coming in with my own bad knee.

We took a four-hour rest at Flathorn Lake. I go by a run-rest rule. The dogs ran four hours from Wasilla to Flathorn Lake, so they needed four hours of rest. That would leave us back in zero-debt mode. Obviously, these dogs are not going to be worn out by a four-hour run. But you have to remember the Iditarod is a marathon. You can do yourself harm for later in the race by going too fast early. You're always planning strategy for a thousand miles. It's discipline. You have to be patient. It's so easy to get too excited and take off. The temptation is to go right on to Skwentna and finish the first 150 miles in one big gulp.

Usually the dogs try to tell you they want to keep running. They bark and fiddle and fuss. They're just being frisky and obnoxious, like little kids who won't stay still when you tell them it's nap time. You wonder, "What am I gaining by stopping?" You have to remind yourself that you have a plan, that there's a reason to stop and you're just being smart for later. This time, a rare time, the dogs lay down and went right to sleep.

In the past, when you came to the cabin of an old friend, or arrived in a village, you could go inside and visit, share a hot meal with a family. Veteran mushers made friends along the trail and stayed with the same families year after year. People considered it an honor to cook a steak dinner for Rick Swenson or to house Susan Butcher. But other mushers complained that such treatment for popular mushers constituted a non-level playing field, that it gave certain mushers an advantage. So the Iditarod officials changed the rules. According to the "corralling" rule, everyone must stay together now in a checkpoint. So we were actually camped in a swamp. It was yucky.

When you are together in one place like that, you also must be careful not to be swayed by someone else's race plan. I had to constantly remind myself, "Yeah, this is where you need to be. Martin left and you are really tempted to go, too, but you have to lie here." It's important to remind yourself that you have a plan and you have to stay with it.

You make a mental note of who you consider the competition to be. You look up when Martin Buser leaves, because he's been a champion, then you remember he left second out of Anchorage and you started twenty-fifth, so he's 50 minutes ahead and he should be leaving first. If you start running someone else's race at this point, it could be a big flaw for you. It takes years to develop the kind of confidence where you can stay put when other mushers are leaving.

A lot of mind games are played between mushers. They try to psyche you out. Someone will say, "That team is dominating the race. Fast team. You can't stay with him."

You have to intimately know the strengths of *your* dog team. And then you have to play *your* dog team's strengths against somebody else's over the course of the entire race.

Endurance was one of the major strengths of my dogs. They could go for hours and hours, and they recovered fast. I tried to keep them from going into any kind of fatigue deficit until very late in the race. They never refused to eat or drink, and that's a great signal of their well-being. When Iditarod dogs are tired, they turn down food and water. They just want to curl up and sleep. I never had that situation.

> "ENDURANCE WAS ONE OF THE MAJOR STRENGTHS OF MY DOGS. THEY COULD GO FOR HOURS AND HOURS, AND THEY RECOVERED FAST."

Speed was not one of our major strengths. We were not the fastest dog team on that trail. But just because we were not the fastest, we could not start running from checkpoint to checkpoint on someone else's schedule.

It took about five hours to mush on to the Skwentna checkpoint. Then we rested five hours, or, I should say, the dogs rested for five hours. I think I got 45 minutes of sleep. You've got to get everything in a camping routine and you'll know when you can sleep. I wasn't in that mode yet. A lot of teams passed me. It's frustrating because you've gotten away from them along the trail, and now you're letting a lot of teams back in while you rest. You can see how easy it would be to give in and go. But if you don't rest, you may over-drive your dog team, and a few days later you'll just be telling yourself you made a stupid mistake.

If I have a style of mushing, it would be to get the best possible performance out of myself and my dogs. If we give our best performance, then let the results fall where they may. I've gone into races and given flawless performances and not won, but been satisfied.

What really upsets me is when I screw up. The dogs don't make mistakes. I make mistakes. I misjudge a situation or make a bad decision. The dogs just listen to me.

On the way to Finger Lake it was spitting snow. It was ugly. I stopped at another swamp and tied the team to a tree. It was quiet there, and I cooked more food for the dogs. When we're out there, I talk to the dogs a lot, softly, in a soothing voice, so they relax. The snow was deep, and every time I walked up the string of dogs my knee hurt. It was really sore.

In the past, I've gone straight through to Finger Lake because I thought we were ready for it. This time I felt we needed this in-between rest. I was a little nervous about that strategy, though, as I watched all the teams go by.

It was only an hour or so until the Finger Lake checkpoint when the dogs decided they deserved another break. Any busy place with race checkers or spectators will lead the dogs to think it might be a rest hangout. I went straight through, though, and it wasn't until then that I realized I was in first place. Everybody else had stayed in Finger Lake. I was so surprised. I thought, "Hey, this works for me. I hadn't even pushed the team at all. We haven't asked for any of the reserves at all yet."

I felt good about it. I was running my own race. I wasn't going by anything Rick Swenson or Susan Butcher were doing. Since Rick has won the race five times and Susan has won it four times, it's easy to get caught up in following them, in thinking they must know what they're doing. But passing through Finger Lake confirmed that I had the right plan for me.

When I left Rainy Pass, I was prepared for the worst. It takes you two days to climb to the pass of the Alaska Range, and it took me about four and a half hours to come down it. This is the danger zone, a rocky trail with hills and exposed areas. It was steep, with a thin coating of snow and some open water. Bad things happen there. I was going down the Dalzell Gorge with full power. The risks were obvious, but for once it turned out to be uneventful negotiating my way along the narrow, downhill trail.

This time there was also glare ice on the Post River. Traveling over glare ice is particularly tricky. Glare ice is a coating of ice so thin that it's difficult to see. It's hard and very slick, and because you haven't spotted it, you might not slow down in advance.

I was trying to get over to the Rohn River, and Elroy, my lead dog, was not used to this. He couldn't find a scratch in the ice for trail. We had a lot of trouble. We wandered back and forth. That was really scary for me. I couldn't hook the team down because there was nothing to grip. I couldn't stop the dogs very easily. I worried about the open water and having no apparent way to command the dogs away from it. It was cloudy, but because it was daylight I could see the trail and where we were supposed to go. That helped me make it safely to Rohn.

On Monday afternoon, a little more than two days into the race, we reached the Rohn checkpoint. Rohn is ringed by mountains and gives me almost a claustrophobic feeling. The valley is deep and kind of dark. There are rocky sandbars coming in and going out. Even though it's a checkpoint, to me it seems more of an outpost than a haven.

There was no snow at all. I had been counting on melting snow for water for the dogs. Now the only way to get water was to hike over to a big ladder, climb down, and dip a bucket in the Rohn River. With my injured knee and hand, this was no fun at all. I didn't need this obstacle. I hadn't had much sleep, I was frustrated, and I was trying to hold it in. I thought, "Okay, okay, this is just what you have to do. This is nobody's fault but our own. It's my hand and my knee. Just one of our shortcomings here."

Leaving Rohn, there was more smooth ice. Ribbons marked the trail, but it was narrow and I didn't want to be the first out. Johnnie, my old leader, could have done it, but I didn't have Johnnie. I wanted these dogs to have at least the scent of another team to follow. Martin Buser finally got ready to go and then Jeff King. I followed them. If the same situation happened again now, I would go out first. Now my dogs have seen the place and they have the experience.

There was a terrible area heading to Farewell Lake. Getting up the glacier on the other side of the Post River is historically very difficult. There was a top layer of ice and even though I had studded boots I just couldn't get up it. The dogs would slide sideways. Rick Swenson came along and we helped each other. My sled got stuck on a lip of ice and he pushed it. I was able to get the team up by hanging on to a rock. Rick's team watched mine and followed closely. We covered 500 yards like this. It was bad.

I was virtually in tears from the pain in my knee, thinking, "Can I get to the next checkpoint?" But you have to contain your frustration and concentrate on the job, because the dogs pick up on it when something's wrong. It isn't their fault you hurt.

This is where I think the Lord really helped me. I just prayed for patience: "Give me patience. Make me kind. Help me be kind." I think the Lord is really where my strength came from to deal with these things.

I took a short break at a new shelter cabin not far from the Sullivan Creek Bridge, still 36 miles from Nikolai. There are 93 miles between Rohn and Nikolai, one of the longest stretches without a checkpoint. But I wasn't planning to take my required 30-hour layover in Nikolai. I wanted to make it to McGrath — which is over 400 miles into the race, and where I had an extra sled, extra clothes, and food waiting for me — before I took that major break.

When I got into Nikolai, I fell to my knees trying to get the team stopped. I was showing the worst wear and tear. So I took a good, long rest there, going to bed for about 90 minutes. I felt lousy, I knew I was just going to have to put up with my body, but I was still there. I just set my mind to do the best I could do. I was encouraged to think that, in spite of what I was working with, we were still in this race.

On the night before the Iditarod began, I had told Mike that I would be happy with anything in the top ten. But by Nikolai, some 365 miles into the race, when I had been over the rough trail and stood up to it, I started thinking differently. I started thinking, "Maybe I can still win. "

When we reached Ophir, my dogs and I bedded down for a nice, long rest.

CHAPTER 3

ALONG
THE TRAIL

I was in first place leaving Takotna, and still in first heading into Ophir. I waited until Ophir, nearly 500 miles into the race, to take my 30-hour mandatory layover. And boy, did I need a break by then. As if I didn't have enough things wrong with me, I got the flu. I guzzled down decongestants and chased them with aspirin.

At that stage of the race, I liked where I was sitting. Every year I race for first, but I want to be top five. If you can consistently be in the top five, you are considered a front-runner and you're taking home enough money to pay the bills. Being in the top five pays $25,000 or more. Teams in the top five are consistently running to win. On any given year, any one of those teams can win. It's the elite corps of the race.

After all of the top teams have taken their 30-hour rest, you really start to get a sense of who you're racing against. All the pre-race talk becomes just that — talk. It's "show me" time. We've made up the stagger from the start times, everyone has had a good rest, and you've seen the speed and endurance of each team.

The first musher who arrives in the ghost town of Iditarod gets a trophy and $3,000 for the halfway award. There is a superstition that the winner of the halfway award never wins the race, but that's silly. It's been done. Not often, but it happens. Dean Osmar did it in 1984. He was ahead, kept control of the race, and kept on going.

What you can't do is disrupt your schedule to chase the halfway prize. That's not wise. Obtaining the award is nice, but it's not the end-all. It didn't fit in with my overall plan. And at that point I was gaining confidence in my race. I was looking at Nome. Still, Jeff King of Denali Park won the award and his team looked terrific. Superstition or not, it was clear he was going to be there for the whole race unless something unusual happened.

After the long rest, my body started to heal. The terrain was smoother, so I wasn't stretching my leg as much and I could ride on the sled runners for longer periods. The medicine was curing my flu. And the weather was mild, very mild for the Iditarod. The temperature was usually above zero. That helped my hand.

One thing I've learned in my years doing the Iditarod is that somewhere along the trail there will be a storm. Usually, it is in the village of Unalakleet, or beyond, when you hit the Bering Sea Coast and are in the final third of the race into Nome.

This time I got hit leaving Iditarod. The wind was blowing, creating a ground blizzard. Swirling snow obliterated the trail. I spent a lot of time looking for the trail markers. Jeff King and Martin Buser were ahead of me and that helped. They did a lot of the hard trail-breaking work. We stayed close together, but the wind was so strong that the trail was almost instantly snowed in after a team passed. It blew for 70 miles, all the way into the village of Shageluk.

We were buffeted all the way by the howling winds. Most of the lead teams needed a rest, but Jeff pressed on to Anvik. He won the first musher to the Yukon award, which pays $3,500 and comes with a fancy seven-course dinner. That's a neat prize, but it's kind of strange. It seems like too much food to swallow after you've been heating up little packets in boiling water and cooking in little pots and pans.

A long race sorts itself out. There's attrition. Susan Butcher was having problems with her dogs. They weren't feeling well. For the first time, I sensed Martin Buser's dogs weren't faster than mine. They were probably moving at the same speed, about eight miles an hour. You take note of these things. You know how fast you can go, but here and there you pick up signs of how fast the others can go. That can be helpful. My dogs looked as good as anybody's at that point.

This is a race where there are no guarantees. You can be cruising one minute and in trouble the next. I have to admit, though, when I left Unalakleet, Shaktoolik, and then White Mountain and was only minutes behind Jeff King, I thought I could win.

It was such an exciting emotion, I almost didn't want to let myself think that. If you start to get confident, you set yourself up for a big disappointment. I've just had too many things go wrong over the 55 miles between White Mountain and Safety. I was not going to allow myself to think that I had the race won unless I was the first musher out of Safety. Then there would be only 22 miles to go.

So on one hand I was high because things were going well. And on the other hand I was getting depressed because I was so tired. It's easy to get depressed on the Iditarod because you are extending yourself and pushing yourself to near exhaustion. The fatigue numbs you and you get down. It's inevitable. So you have to discipline your mood swings, to figure out reality and stay on an even keel. I use music to help. I listen to my Walkman.

On the trail I played a tape made for me by friends at the Big Lake Baptist Church, where Mike and I are members. I'd crank it up and think of things that make me happy. There are some great, victorious songs on there and my friend Marietta has a beautiful voice. She spoke to me, encouraged me, on the tape. It was very uplifting. I also prayed, "Please Lord, give me a better spirit than I have now."

Basically, my husband Mike and I are pretty happy people. We don't get too shook by things. We have our foundation down. I just want Mike to be pleased with me. And as long as I'm doing my best, he is. He would be more upset with me for getting distraught and discouraged than he would if I finished in thirty-fifth place. Of course, he'd love it if I won, but he's going to help me and support me no matter what.

In 1993, with all my aches, Mike had trained the dogs more than ever. I train them 100 percent of the time during the dryland training, but when the snow falls, Mike can be contributing 50 percent of the training time to help me.

He told me before the 1993 race, "I don't want you to go out and do this just because you think you owe it to me for the time I spent training the team. I don't want you to ruin your knee for one race. I want you to withdraw if you think you're going to wreck your knee. It isn't worth it."

It was comforting to hear him say that, but I also did want him to feel proud of me. I knew I just had to give it my best effort.

For me, the section between Grayling and Kaltag, just before you reach the villages of the coast, is often discouraging. It seems as if you've been out on the trail forever — it's been a week — and there's still a lot of racing to go. The distances are so great from the start and from the end.

Coming into Grayling there was all this confusing activity. Snowmachines were buzzing around. "What is this?" I thought. I was so lost in my thoughts that I'd completely lost track of the race. This action surrounding me was because I was the first musher in! That will lift your spirits, finding out you're running in first place.

It was amazing. There were tons of kids and they wanted autographs. An older Athabaskan woman, Eleanor Deacon, approached me as I was bedding down the dogs. She asked, "Can I give you this for being the first to Grayling?" And she gave me a birch basket. These are the great moments in the Iditarod, when you meet the people and they make you feel so special. I heard later she said to someone, "Do you think she came first to Grayling for the basket?" I sure didn't know there was a basket there, but it was well worth it. I was very, very touched.

The checker there was Joe Maille, an old friend from Bethel who I only see on the trail every couple of years now. There were big hugs all around from him and his daughter and wife. All this totally changed my mood. How can you not have your spirits raised with a greeting like that? I felt I was in control again.

I took a nine-hour rest and when we mushed out of town so did Jeff. We stayed pretty close, within a few hundred yards or a half mile of each other, and I could tell that Jeff was faster. Maybe only a half mile per hour faster, but definitely faster. Not a good sign, but not a fatal sign.

Jeff and I pulled out together toward Kaltag. After 22 miles, the wind was whipping. I was still racing sixteen dogs, a big team; that helped me because that's good power to be driving. There were no other mushers with us, but Rick Mackey was hovering behind us. He still had nineteen dogs and was about an hour and a half back.

It was time to pull the plug on the strict run-rest mode. We couldn't afford to avoid deficit running. There comes a time when you must go longer. With some 350 miles to go at that point, you either hang in there or you fade. It's a gamble, but if you don't do it, you won't be there at the finish anyway.

I was in first between Kaltag and Unalakleet for four hours and I was surprised. I didn't see Jeff King until the Old Woman cabin. But he did catch me — and he pulled away on the flats. That was a reminder of how strong his dogs were.

I rested for a couple of hours before Susan Butcher and Martin Buser came in. Rick Mackey cruised right through without bother-

Crowds around the finish chute welcomed me into Nome.

ing to stop and he did look tough. It was the first time he had passed us. Martin said, "Congratulations, 1993 winner, race well run."

That's how you can get psyched out. Martin's implication was that the rest of us were all just running for second. Jeff and I looked at each other, and Jeff said, "I think I'm still faster than him. And I'm not willing to concede this yet."

I decided that I didn't care if Jeff beat me or if Rick Mackey won the race, but I wanted a personal best finish. That meant I had to be third at least. I didn't care about my knee or my hand anymore.

I planned to rest in Unalakleet, but the village was excited, the kids were jumping around, and the dogs weren't resting. The other mushers went on. So I made a race move. I adjusted to the moment.

I had to go or I was no longer really part of the race. So I moved out again.

The hesitation cost me a little bit. Rick and Jeff arrived in Shaktoolik a half hour ahead of me. Just because you make a mistake, though, you can't let it shatter you. I thought, "I can make it up somewhere else. I can deal with this."

My head was all fuzzy in Shaktoolik. I hadn't slept since Grayling, and I wanted a three-hour nap. I lay down on the floor of this trailer next to Mackey, but a couple of hours later someone woke me and said Jeff was going. I said, "What's Rick doing?" Rick was sleeping next to me! I woke him and said, "Jeff's going." He said, "What's DeeDee doing?" I said, "I'm DeeDee. I'm waking you up!" We ended up going back to sleep for another hour. When we mushed out, Rick said, "I hope we didn't blow it."

I wasn't too worried because at that moment I thought I was racing for third. But my dogs were so strong and were moving so well. At Koyuk, which is close to 1,000 miles into the race, I figured I'd sacrifice rest to leave with Jeff. I was one hour, twenty minutes behind. The ABC-TV reporter tried to get me to say that was too much to catch up. I wouldn't. I said, "I just simply will not concede this race at Koyuk."

By Elim, another 50 miles down the trail, the three of us — me, Jeff, and Rick — were strung out like the cars in a freight train. I could see them at all times. I blew off rest and watering the dogs in Elim; instead I just threw them a snack. I carry fish, lamb, salmon, and whitefish, things to give them encouragement. At one point I passed both Rick and Jeff. Then Rick had to drop a dog. That was significant. It was a sign of his team faltering, a chink in his armor, something I might be able to capitalize on.

When you reach White Mountain, there are only 77 miles to Nome. I had closed to seven minutes behind Jeff. When ABC interviewed me that time, I said, "Seven minutes. It's a different

©1994 JEFF SCHULTZ

First-place finisher Jeff King and I shared a hug after the race.

game now." We had 12 hours to recover. If my dogs recouped, we could win. Mackey was an hour behind me. Things were sorting themselves out.

Neither Jeff nor I had ever won the Iditarod. He said to me, "You're not who I thought I would be racing. Isn't it interesting how things change? But it's you and me for first and second." I said, "Either way, that's great." Jeff said, "Either way."

Something good was going to happen, no matter how it turned out. I knew the team wasn't fading. Whether we were going to be able to beat Jeff, I didn't know. I could only dream of what it would be like to come in first.

My heart jumped and my stomach fluttered. I almost started crying. I thought of Elroy and Bristol, the dogs in lead, and how hard they had worked. I thought about them as a parent would.

If you win the Iditarod, not only do you get $50,000, but you win a Dodge truck, too, and Mike could have used that truck. I thought about how I would cross the finish line, turn to my husband, and say, "Michael, this is from the team. We thank you for your efforts." Then I would give him the keys to the truck.

I had never before imagined what winning would be like in such detail. Jeff left White Mountain seven minutes before me, and for the first 30 or so miles I had him in sight. Then I lost him in the Topkok Hills, about 40 miles from the finish. I never stopped moving, but he was faster. You never give up. You can't underestimate the things that can go wrong.

But nothing went wrong for Jeff. It was shortly after midnight when Jeff finished with a new record time of 10 days, 15 hours, 38 minutes. I was a half hour behind him. And I was truly exhausted when my dogs mushed under the burled arch on Front Street.

The crowds were huge. That was exciting. But my knee hurt, my hand hurt, everything hurt. I said I couldn't wait to take the knee bandage off, that it would be like letting my knee out of jail.

I was disappointed at being second, yet it was more of a peaceful feeling than I thought it would be. In many ways I had greatly exceeded our expectations. It was the second fastest Iditarod of all time. It was my best time and my best finish. I won $43,000. Also, it was my most dogs, thirteen, at the finish.

Jeff King was a great winner. To have the second best performance ever to Jeff was nothing to be ashamed of.

One of my goals is to be a positive influence on people's lives.

CHAPTER 4

IN THE SPOTLIGHT

The finish was wonderful. Crowds lined Front Street and everyone was cheering. Nome celebrates the end of the Iditarod with the same vigor as New Yorkers celebrate New Year's in Times Square.

No matter whether it's day or night, thousands of people greet the winner and other top finishers. It's the biggest event of the year in the old gold rush community. When I mushed down Front Street it was late at night — closing in on 1 a.m. — but that didn't matter. I didn't care about the hour, and the fans didn't seem to know what time it was, either. I felt so happy to be there, to be finished after the long trip, it might as well have been a sunny afternoon.

What a wonderful reception. And that was just the start. As soon as I got home, the mail poured in, a lot of it from school kids around the country. Hundreds and hundreds of letters. People wrote to me who I hadn't seen in years. They just wanted to tell me they saw me on television and were rooting for me. I got a lot of "atta-girls."

Something about the way I finished the race, overcoming all my health hazards, must have touched people. Many girls and women contacted me to tell me that I was an inspiration to them because I was a woman who was having success. A lot of younger girls, from first grade to high school, wrote to me and said they really loved animals, but they didn't know if they could do something like race in the Iditarod. They asked me for advice. I sent out autographs and pictures, but also tried to offer them a little more than that. You want kids to understand you appreciate their interest and their support. You tell them to hang in there.

I was in demand in many ways after the race. At the Eddie Bauer store in Anchorage, I made a four-hour appearance, signing autographs. Even though he wasn't my leader anymore, I brought Johnnie because he's so good with people. Only he shed all over the place. There was plenty of hair to go around.

We brought pictures to give out, and I signed 250 of them. The store had our DeeDee Jonrowe team sweatshirts, and I was asked to sign those. It's a challenge to sign your name on an all-black sweatshirt.

I enjoy sessions like that, meeting and talking to people. Getting out in public is important and the spring is a good time for that. You're fresh off the race, and it's a rest and recovery time, both for you and the dogs. Public appearances are the best way for people to gain a better comprehension of the Iditarod and dog mushing in general. There is a lot of misinformation being spread about dog mushing by opponents of the Iditarod, people who say that mushers are indifferent to the fate of their dogs and are sloppy in taking care of them. I like public forums which give me the chance to set people straight.

Still, I am always very tired when I finish an appearance like that. I try to put my all into it, to be nice to everyone, but it's tough to be on stage constantly for four hours straight. I can't imagine what life must be like for a Hollywood star or a big sports star like Michael Jordan. Wow.

In the next few weeks, I spoke at a symposium given by the Alaska Women of the Wilderness at the University of Alaska Anchorage, and I participated in a print-signing with the artist Penni Ann Cross, who is musher Joe Garnie's wife. After the print-signing, I went to Seattle to visit Eddie Bauer's offices.

In five days, I think I met every single Eddie Bauer employee — and there are thousands of them. My first day there began at 5:30 a.m. I did interviews with three television stations, four radio stations, and two newspapers, and I visited an elementary school. And then I was on TV again that night doing a local news magazine show. While I was there, I also did four slide shows for people at the corporate offices, and another show at a dog food distributor in Renton. This is one way you pay back sponsors who take care of you and support you while you're preparing for the Iditarod.

Both before and after my trip to Seattle, I was invited to speak at several local Alaska churches. I like to make those appearances. Usually, I speak for about twenty minutes, talking about how my race unfolded, my commitment to racing and my faith, and how my faith has played a major role in my career.

If winning is the only reason you are out on the Iditarod Trail, then you are going to be disappointed for many, many years. If your goal is to do your best and be a positive influence in people's lives, then you can be a winner every year. The Lord has been a big motivator for me, and has helped me keep my perspective in what I do.

The top priority in my life is to be the best I can be wherever the Lord wants me to do service. A lot of people think if you're going to influence people's lives, you have to live your religion by becoming a missionary in Africa, but I don't believe that's the case. I believe the Lord has a purpose for me as a Christian dog musher. There are not that many Christian dog mushers. In fact, if you think about it, there are fewer Christian dog mushers than there are missionaries in Africa.

To me, living my faith is about being an upright, upstanding citizen. I try to act out my beliefs in daily life. One of the Christian songs on the tape I played during the 1993 race was called, "In Christ there are no losers." There's only going to be one first-place finisher in each year's race, but I think there are lots of winners. People win in different ways.

Each musher has different things he or she overcomes. Mushers win in the manner in which they take care of their dogs, in the way they treat people they meet in the villages, and in how courteous they are to volunteers. They win by acting in a way that can have a good effect on some child's life. Mushers can have a good influence even by what they say in interviews or by answering letters from fans. There are many ways to win in the Iditarod.

Later in the year, I was the speaker at a baccalaureate ceremony at West High in Anchorage, then gave the commencement address at nearby Houston High School. The theme of both my talks was built around a biblical passage from Isaiah: "Even the strong grow weary and the young men grow tired, but they that live in the Lord will rise up with strength like eagles. They will run and not be weary."

A friend of mine, Willard Potter, sent that to me to perk me up when I was mushing through White Mountain during the 1993 Iditarod. Another guy from the Covenant Church also brought it down to the checkpoint to me. They picked that passage because of all the difficulties I had in the race, with all of my injuries, and all that I had to overcome. Certainly, there was little rational explanation for why things worked out so successfully, except that I kept trying. I believe that you can't let circumstances stop you. If you've got a vision, pursue your vision. Don't let the circumstances that arise prevent you from going on. That was the message I wanted to get across to the students.

Soon after the high school speeches, I was invited to participate in the Alaska Special Olympics opening ceremonies in Anchorage. I didn't really have any major obligation or role, but I wanted to be there as a show of support for Special Olympics. It's an amazing event that brings out the best in so many people.

The Special Olympics provide sports participation opportunities for the physically and mentally disabled, and you can't help but be reminded how lucky you are. You think, "There but by the grace of God go I." You also can't help but think that your own complaints and injuries are so petty by comparison. I thought, "Oh well, my knee hurt during the Iditarod. But what if I never had the use of my knee?" Some of the people have serious handicaps, yet they are very supportive of one another. Going to the Special Olympics is quite a lesson in sportsmanship.

As the year went on, my sport would take me all over the world. Since Royal Canin, the dog food makers, is one of my main sponsors, I travel to France for a major meeting each year. I'm part of the Royal Canin international racing team. The company sponsors mushers in Norway, Germany, Finland, Italy, Holland, France, and in the United States — me. The idea is that Royal Canin has mushers from different countries who race under different conditions and experience different things. Then we come together annually to share our training progams, our ideas, and what happened to us during the year. We compare notes on our nutritional successes and failures. We say, "I did this race and this is what happened." This provides Royal Canin with a field test of their products.

In October, I traveled to Canada to speak to a fledgling mushing club. I had been under the impression that I was going to be a small part of the program, but it turned out when I got there that I was the program! I ended up speaking for eight and a half hours. I tried to cram as much as I possibly could into one day. I wanted to make sure the mushers had something new or exciting to try with their nutrition, or their breeding, or their training, just so somehow they could look at their dogs in a new light. I talked about equipment. I gave demonstrations about harnesses and how they should fit. I was a teacher imparting my wisdom acquired from years of racing the Iditarod. By offering information, I might save them from making some of the mistakes I made along the way.

Now I like to talk and I love to explain dog mushing to people, but talking for more than eight straight hours set some kind of personal record. I was a serious candidate for laryngitis.

In November I made time for a trip to McGrath to be part of a country gospel singing weekend. McGrath is a community of about 500 people in the Interior, about 400 miles along the Iditarod Trail. It serves as a race checkpoint, but, of course, when you're racing you don't have much time to hang out. During the race, someone has to hold the kids back and keep them away from the dogs and everyone is tired.

I was glad to go there to talk with the people and spend time. I brought mushers' cards with me; we have trading cards like baseball cards. It's important to give something back to the communities along the trail. They help us when we need them, but you're not at your best when you're mushing through on the fly, on no sleep, worrying about the competition.

Racing sled dogs is a selfish occupation. To be in the front of the pack, you have to be self-centered. You've got to be focused, thinking more about your dogs than about any human beings. The dogs come before your husband and your family, especially during the race.

That's fine for race week. But I've also decided that you must balance your life or you're going to lose your marriage and your friends and family. You must make time for other people. Mushing can't be all take, take, take. Part of winning is having your life in balance, giving something from your success to other people.

I remember one cute little girl who came up to me in Shageluk during the 1993 Iditarod. She said, "I want to be a dog musher." I said, "Well, honey, when you graduate from college, you go right ahead. It's a great thing to do, but get your college degree first."

I feel it is my responsibility to be a role model, to conduct my life properly 365 days a year. I don't think that anything goes just because I'm away from the trail. If I'm recognized in the grocery store behaving poorly, it will leave a bad impression. People remember. That may be the only time they see me.

I try to have good health habits, too. I'm not a drinker. I'm not a smoker. That's just good sense. I want to help my dogs, not hinder them. I have to be in good shape for mushing. And if people saw me in a bar, they would talk: "Hey, look, isn't that DeeDee Jonrowe? She's smashed." I don't want to be seen like that.

If I am considered a role model, that's fine. I don't shirk that designation. I am also behaving in a certain way to be true to myself. This is the standard by which I choose to live, the values I have. It all goes hand-in-hand with being in the public eye. I chose to enter the Iditarod, and I have to take the responsibility that comes with that.

When I was five years old, I took riding lessons in Ethiopia.

CHAPTER 5

GROWING UP IN A DOG FAMILY

W hen I was a kid, I was just like that little girl I met in Shageluk. I loved dogs. Of course, I had no idea what a dog musher was.

I was born December 20, 1953, at a military hospital in Frankfurt, Germany, to Army parents. My father, Ken Stout, now a retired lieutenant colonel, was stationed in Greece at the time.

The Army brought us to Alaska — eventually. We didn't live anywhere very long when I was growing up. I started school in Ethiopia. My junior high years were spent in Okinawa, and I graduated from high school in Virginia, not far from Washington, D.C.

We were a dog family. We had a long line of German shepherds. We've had everything. We've adopted from animal shelters. We've had Pekinese. We've had a hodge-podge of different kinds of dogs and now my house dogs are Labrador retrievers.

I've always had pets. If I was in between dogs for one reason or another, I had a cat. When I was little, I even had guinea pigs that I dressed up instead of dolls.

Looking back on it, I think my mother used pets to teach values to my younger sister Linda and me. My mom is from northern Virginia, and my dad is from Missouri. They both grew up on farms and were both animal lovers. By caring for our pets, we were taught to be loving and unselfish, to share, and to put a living thing before our own more selfish interests. It was a good way to learn responsibility. Children have a tendency to be rough, and we were taught to be kind and gentle, right off the bat. I remember those lessons today when I deal with my sled dogs.

My family moved to Alaska after I finished high school. My dad had been assigned to Fort Richardson in Anchorage. I was seventeen, and the coldest place I'd ever been was Massachusetts. I was scared of the cold. I knew nothing at all about Alaska except that it snowed a lot. I thought it was just going to be awful. Hah. Here I am, more than 23 years later, and I love it. But then I liked horses, and I was going to have to get rid of my horse when we moved north. I liked warm weather and farms and beaches. I wanted to be a dairy farmer. Well, I was right about one thing: it does snow a lot in Alaska.

My father told me I could go to college anyplace in Alaska, so my choices were the University of Alaska Anchorage or the University of Alaska Fairbanks. I didn't want to live at home, so I chose Fairbanks. I started at UAF in 1971.

One bad thing about being in the dormitory at UAF was the rule against having large pets. I was not able to have a dog, so I got guinea pigs again. Sometimes, bending the regulations a little bit, I'd bring a stray dog in to spend the night. It drove my roommate nuts. It was difficult for me to be without a dog or cat. I was so used to having one that I missed the companionship of an animal. Of course, at that age, when you're just beginning college, it's a difficult time anyway. You're trying to fit in and find your peer group. Having a dog would have been comforting.

Originally, I wanted to go to veterinary school, but Alaska

didn't have one. I took as many pre-veterinary courses as I could, but I could see that it wasn't going to work out, and I eventually studied wildlife management.

It seems so strange to think back to my early years in Fairbanks. I had never been in the cold, and I just screamed when I looked at the thermometer and saw it was 70 below. Seventy below zero! I was amazed anyone could exist in such cold temperatures. And now, in the Iditarod, I not only exist in weather like that, but I make progress. We'll get hit by storms that have a windchill factor of 100 degrees below zero, and we mush on.

But the winter was also beautiful: the snow, the trees. Alaska is probably the most beautiful place on earth and I understood that right away my freshman year in college. Fairbanks was so fresh to me, so untamed. There were a lot of new things to see and do. The people were adventuresome, a bit on the wild side. I never thought of myself that way before, but I was attracted to that. By spring I was cross-country skiing on glaciers down the highway near Delta. I started going out when it was 60 below.

It was harder to get used to the darkness than the cold. Fairbanks is nearly 400 miles north of Anchorage. Even though it's not above the Arctic Circle, it's far enough north that at the end of December, around the Winter Solstice, it only gets a couple of hours of daylight. It was dark so much that I felt like sleeping fourteen hours a day. As a way to combat that inclination, I tried to get involved in more activities, and I joined the college basketball team. I was already my full height of 5' 2", so naturally I played guard. They were not going to put me at center.

In fact, basketball indirectly led me to racing the Iditarod. Every year, coinciding with the finish of the race, there is a huge basketball tournament in Nome. Teams come from all around the state to compete. When I was in Nome for the tournament with a team from Bethel in 1979, I watched Rick Swenson win the Iditarod.

The finish was at night. He mushed his team under the burled arch, and he jumped up to touch the crosspiece. The dogs looked good and strong and for some reason I started crying. I was so touched and so amazed and so impressed by the dogs. My emotions welled up. I thought about the awesomeness of what Rick had just accomplished, mushing more than 1,100 miles. I could see the joy he felt in his heart, and the determination. The picture of that scene stayed with me forever.

Several years before that, when I was still attending school in Fairbanks, I'd had a sled dog ride. John Cooper, a top Iditarod musher in the 70s and 80s, was dating a girlfriend of mine. They stayed with me and my boyfriend, and one day they weren't around, so I thought I'd just hook the dogs up. I had seen huskies in the movies and at the North American Sprint Championships, so I thought I knew what to do. I could just taste it, how much fun and how exciting it would be to take a ride.

I did not know what I was doing. I put the harnesses on the dogs, but they got all tangled up. The dogs started to run, I fell off the back of the sled, and the dogs disappeared. I had been on the sled less than five minutes. I was stunned, and at first I was scared to even tell anyone what happened. It took two days to get the dogs back. They were found across town from the university, over by Fort Wainwright.

That was a brief ride, indeed, but my interest in dog mushing grew over time. My father had a friend, Walt Palmer, who had a team and he let me drive his five dogs around Christmas of 1978. I pumped Walt for information, then borrowed some dogs and entered the 1979 Anchorage Fur Rendezvous Women's World Championship, a three-day sprint race held in February every year. That was my first dog race.

I discovered very quickly I was not as familiar with dogs as I thought I was. I was idealistic and enthusiastic, but I wasn't a racer.

These dogs weren't very well-behaved. They weren't responsive. On the first day of the race, they were fighting and I pulled over to get them to stop. They darted off the trail, ran towards Tudor Road, which is thickly traveled by automobiles, and flipped me off the runners.

I knew enough not to let go of the sled, so they dragged me out to the main street on my face. I was dragged down four lanes of traffic until somebody finally caught the lead dogs and pulled them off to the side of the road. All the buttons on my coat were sanded off.

I was forced out of the race after only about four miles. But I told my mother right then I'd be back, and when I raced again it would be with my own dogs. I bought five dogs while I was in Anchorage, and I brought them home with me. The next time I entered a dog race, I would be ready.

By then I was living in Bethel, where I would spend thirteen of the most significant years of my life. Bethel, which is located in southwest Alaska in the Kuskokwim Delta, was a community of about 2,500 mostly Eskimo people when I first went there in the spring of 1974. It was a free, easy place that offered wide opportunities to be whatever you wanted to be.

Of course, in many ways, all of Alaska was like that. There were so many animal-related and outdoor opportunities. At UAF I had taken every class I could in wildlife management. In those classes, there would be only two or three girls and the professors would always say, "Oh, there's no jobs for women in this field." I just ignored what they said and kept at it. "I will study what I want to study," I thought.

It turned out that when I finished school, they were building the trans-Alaska pipeline to carry the oil from Prudhoe Bay to Valdez, so there were job opportunities for women in many fields. After I graduated in three years, I went to work for the state Department of Fish and Game in Bethel. I was a fisherman's technician, a fisher biologist, actually. I was a commercial catch monitor. I took scale samples for studies and I tabulated the number of fish brought in by boats, primarily king salmon and chums from the Kuskokwim River. All the counting was done by hand in those days.

I met Mike that first year. He had worked for Fish and Game for a number of years already. We were co-workers and I stayed in Bethel for six months. It was seasonal work. My first couple of years, I spent only the fishing season in Bethel, but I began living there year-round in 1976.

Mike and I got married in 1977, and for several years we lived in a condemned trailer. It was really cold and it was very, very small. There was no place in the trailer you could not hold hands. But we were young and in love and happy. The trailer was dilapidated, but okay. When state officials figured out we were living in it and they owned it, they decided they might have to charge rent for it. So we said, "If you are going to charge us rent, how about all the things that go along with it?" Our landlords decided the trailer was beyond repair and they just bulldozed it.

It doesn't sound pretty, but when you're a young married couple just starting out, you look at things differently. In the early days of our marriage in Bethel, we went to the office and went out snowmachining, or ptarmigan hunting, or cross-country skiing on the tundra. We weren't in the trailer very much anyway.

If I thought Alaska was the land of opportunity, where you could establish your own identity doing whatever you wanted, Bethel took that a step further. Bethel was not a major metropolis. If you had skills of any sort, you could use them to help out. For a while I was a radio announcer on the public broadcasting station. I played whatever music I wanted, read the news, and passed on messages. In Bush Alaska, many people live in isolated cabins and they don't have telephones. One way people communicate is by contacting the radio station and asking them to read messages on the air. This was called "Tundra Drums," like a message being passed through the beating of a drum. We did it four times a day. They were pretty wide-ranging messages. A lot of them were pleas: "We miss you, please come home," or "I think I left my wedding dress under the bed in my house. Can you send it to me?" It was fascinating.

"I FELL IN LOVE WITH MUSHING. . . . ON THE OPEN TUNDRA, IT WAS BEAUTIFUL, SO BEAUTIFUL."

I tried out lots of things. I worked in the school system with special education kids. I also taught history and biology at the community college. I was Bethel's first animal control officer. I worked for the public works department doing the original numbering for the residences. At one point, I had four or five part-time jobs simultaneously. That was a real experience. I eventually realized I couldn't stay awake that many hours of the day.

When I first got to Bethel, snowmachines were the main mode of transportation. There were a few dog teams around, but they were work dogs who hauled wood. There were no race dogs. Nobody cared about racing. There is a long tradition of spring carnival racing in many villages of Interior Alaska, but there was no racing at all in Bethel.

Myron Angstman, a lawyer in Bethel, had some dogs, and so did a few families in the villages. A little surge of mushing interest began when Myron did the Iditarod in 1979. He finished twenty-fifth, but when he came home there was so much enthusiasm about it. Myron took advantage of that to organize the Kuskokwim 300, and today it is one of the premier middle-distance races in the world.

When Mike and I first got some dogs, the plan was just to have a recreational team. It was going to be a fun way to look around Bethel's environs, to mush to some of the nearby villages and visit friends. I just fell in love with mushing. Most of my travel was done in the spring, and it was sunny weather, with temperatures in the 30s. On the open tundra, it was beautiful, so beautiful.

By the fall of 1979, I had twenty dogs. I just collected them one by one. Mike was out of town on business and I was talking to a friend. We decided I should run the Iditarod. I figured, "Why not?" And I sent my entry fee in.

To me it didn't seem like all that big a leap. I was mushing around, and I just decided I wanted to race with the dogs. I'm competitive. For me, part of the fun of anything I do is making it a competition.

I really didn't have any idea what participating in the Iditarod was going to be like, though. I'd seen parts of it. I'd seen Myron practice for it. But I was really ignorant. Knowing what I know now, I would not have done it right then. I didn't know the country and didn't have the experience.

My debut in long-distance racing was actually the 1980 Kusko 300. Boy, did I have lots of problems.

I didn't know how to feed the dogs. I had gear falling off the sled all over the place. I took too much gear, which is a common mistake made by rookies in long races, and I had things roped all over the sled instead of neatly stowed in a sled basket. I didn't even have a tarp over the pile. It was like those old western movies, when you see covered wagons with all the junk hanging off the sides. This was learning by winging it.

On the first day of the Kusko, I was mushing about 15 miles out of the village of Tuluksak, only 50 or so miles north of Bethel, when we were hit by a bad storm. The dogs wouldn't go forward or backward; they just lay down. It was a blizzard with no visibility. There was a windchill factor of minus 50. My feet were really, really cold, but at the time I was more worried about the safety of the dogs than my own health.

Race officials tried two or three times to find me with rescue crews and were unable to because the snowmachines couldn't get through the drifts. I just gathered the dogs around me to try to stay warm and prayed that we would get out of it. I was saying, "Oh my God, if I ever get out of this alive, I'll never do this again."

I was stuck there right by the trail for 36 hours. Eventually, I was able to mush the dogs back into Tuluksak.

At this point, my mushing career had consisted of getting dragged through the streets of Anchorage on my face and getting clobbered by a storm. I'd be lying if I said I didn't have some worries about my first Iditarod. But I'd paid my entry fee: $600. I think if it had been easy to withdraw, I would have. But it wasn't easy to do that. Also, nobody in my family wanted me to go. That fact made me even more determined to finish the Iditarod.

Equipped with a headlamp and a furry hat, I entered my first Iditarod in 1980.

CHAPTER 6

IDITAROD DEBUT

I'm glad you only have to be a rookie in the Iditarod once.
That lack of confidence you have — of never having been
through the race, of never having covered 1,100 miles on the
sled, of not being sure what happens next — means that you're
scared, that there's adrenalin flowing through you all the time.
That's what my 1980 debut in the Iditarod was like.

My mom and dad really didn't want me to start the race. They
made comments like, "You're not ready," and "Maybe this isn't such
a good idea." Both of those things were true.

It never dawned on me that it was something I wouldn't be able
to accomplish, though. I never thought I was wasting my money,
because I never thought I wouldn't be able to finish. I did think once
I completed the Iditarod it would be the only time, however. I never
expected to be a perennial runner.

From the beginning I had a sense that none of the other
mushers took me seriously. My attitude was "I'll show you guys." It
is different being a woman in a male-dominated sport. Dog mushing
is one of the few sports in the world where women and men compete
as equals. But especially in the early days of the Iditarod, it wasn't

clear to women that they were accepted.

By becoming a top contender, Susan Butcher made the real breakthrough for women at the front of the pack, but it had to be a bit of a lonely existence for a while. When Libby Riddles won the Iditarod in 1985, she was the first woman to do so, but by that time Susan had created the climate where the public expected a woman would win. Now everyone expects women to be contenders.

Susan paved the way. She finished in the top ten for the first time in 1979 and, of course, she won the race four times after that. Susan and I were good friends when I started racing. She helped me a lot and really encouraged me. In her first Iditarods, Susan said she was always on the outside of the campfire and didn't really feel included when mushers stopped to rest. I understood what she was saying and we built a mutual companionship as the women racing every year. Nobody knew what it was like to be out there except her and me. If you spend ten or eleven days out on the trail, even if you only do it once a year, you've got something special going. You have something with one special friend and nobody else. We were competing, but we could still bounce our happiness or sadness off each other.

Women were still a novelty in the Iditarod when I first entered, though there were eight women in the field of sixty-one mushers. The difference now is that more women are closer to the front. In 1993, when I finished second, Susan finished fourth. But there were also three other women in the top twenty.

The latest craze among certain male mushers is to say women have it easier because they weigh less and their dogs are carrying less weight along the trail. That's ridiculous. How well the dogs do is mostly attributable to their training. The race is the culmination of the entire training program of the animals, as well as their nutrition, medical care, and athletic ability. Weight is just one small element.

I'm a small person, and there are times on the trail when being bigger, having more upper body strength, would be an advantage. One place is in the Farewell Burn. You have to sidehill and you can slip under a tree if you don't have the power to control the sled. Your ability to run with the dogs uphill is another piece of the pie. Some mushers are better runners. I think those things even out on the trail.

In all my years of racing, I never picked up on any kind of anti-woman sentiment from fans. In earlier races, before I was established, I did experience nastiness from male mushers in the Iditarod. A lot of times men wouldn't even talk to me. Other times they would say, "What are you doing out here?" It was as if they were saying a woman's place is in the home. It hurts your feelings. I wonder if some men thought it was an infringement on their masculinity, that their idea of being a rough, tough outdoor-type was being challenged because women were proving they could be tough in the Iditarod, too.

This shouldn't sound as if it applies to the majority of male mushers — it doesn't. Most of the guys were great. I wouldn't be where I am in the Iditarod today if guys didn't help me in my first race.

The winter before my first race, Joe Redington, the Father of the Iditarod, stayed with Mike and I in Bethel. Joe encouraged me and taught me stuff about feeding and how to pack the sled. Mushers always say, "If you take care of your dogs, they will take good care of you." That was never a problem for me. That came naturally from a lifetime of having pets. I knew when a dog was tired or thirsty, when a dog was happy or unhappy. I did not know the intricate details and ways of feeding in a race situation. Joe taught me the basics.

Still, on the first night of my first Iditarod in March, 1980, I was terrified. Absolutely terrified.

I was traveling up the Skwentna River. I stopped for four hours to rest the dogs, about midnight, maybe 80 miles into the race, and

I parked right on the trail. One of the things Joe had told me was that there was only one main trail. Boy, did I remember that, and I wouldn't leave the trail. I just thought if I moved an inch off the trail, I'd end up mushing in circles and be lost forever.

People were passing me and they had things to say to me because I was in their way. I didn't care what they said to me because I was scared and I wasn't going to leave the trail and get lost. My experience in the Kusko 300 was haunting me.

After Flathorn Lake, out on the frozen river, the guy in front of me lost his team. And then I lost my team for a second. That was my nightmare come true. I fell off the sled backwards, but somebody grabbed my team before it could get away.

Myron Angstman had told me that no matter how bad anything got, it would only last a short while, so I could live with it. "Keep going forward," he said. I kept reminding myself of that.

All of my mushing experience had been on the flat tundra, out near Bethel, and now I was on rivers and hills. My dogs didn't know anything about going up mountains. When I went down the hill to Happy River, it was so steep that the dogs didn't want to go up the other side. I had to crawl up the hill in front and pull the dogs and the sled up myself. It was a terrible chore.

At the summit of Rainy Pass, I couldn't believe we were a few thousand feet up. It seemed impossibly high. I started to get discouraged, and that's where a couple of veteran mushers, Don Honea and Rudy Demoski, befriended me.

Until then I was just barely making my way. Those guys chided me and cajoled me. They teased me to push me a little bit. I needed that. I hadn't been traveling at their speed, but I stayed with them for 18 hours. They built my confidence back up.

And then I had a dog die.

Her name was Venus, and she was one of five dogs I'd had for a year. As we were cresting at Rainy Pass, the dogs were running and she just went down. I threw my snow hook in and by the time I reached her, she was already dead. It was that quick. It turned out she had a faulty valve in her heart.

I was crying and crying. It was a great trauma. "What am I going to do now? What am I doing here? What did I do wrong?" I blamed myself and wanted to quit the race.

I was paralyzed by what had happened. Rudy tried to shock me into regaining my senses. He said, "Why are you so stupid? You can't stop. Get on the sled and get going." He later said I was so upset all he could do was get mad. He said he knew empathizing was not the way to get me going.

At the time I thought, "You're so mean." But he shocked me out of my grief. Until you've lost an animal you care about, you can't understand the pain and frustration. The dogs are not disposable. They are not just interchangeable parts. I love my dogs. That was the only dog I have ever lost racing the Iditarod.

After that, I was very conservative on the trail. I rested the dogs a lot. I didn't push them hard.

Of course, my sled was loaded with junk I didn't need. That's a typical rookie mistake. You plan for every eventuality, but you really don't know what those eventualities are until you've been out there. What you have to learn is the right stuff to bring, so you don't have too much of one thing and not enough of another thing. I brought everything but the kitchen sink. I dumped a lot of stuff along the way.

Venus's death distracted me, and it took nearly a week for me to get over it and enjoy the race again. I began to have some fun when I hit the village of Ruby, which is about 650 miles into the race. Ruby is the first checkpoint on the Yukon River and it's an old gold-mining community. Only a few hundred people live there. When I got there, the temperature was about 20 below. My dogs liked the cold and this is where they showed me they still had it. I should have known things would go well there, since my best leader that year was also named Ruby.

My mind cleared with the cold. I started to think competitively, to think like a racer. I was back in my element. Ruby felt like Bethel to me. The people were wonderful, and Ruby is beautiful. Once you are on the frozen Yukon River, you are going from village to village. You look forward to seeing new people and being greeted with enthusiasm at regular intervals. In between, the country is gorgeous.

After Kaltag, on the way into Unalakleet, I really felt at home. Here the race turns to the Bering Sea Coast and the terrain is flat. It felt just like the tundra around Bethel. On the horizon, Unalakleet even looked like Bethel, and that made me happy. Every year it strikes me that way, but it made all the difference in the world in my attitude that first year. From then on my spirits were way up. Traveling from Kaltag to Unalakleet that year was one of the stretches I'd like to think I'll keep as a memory forever.

Even after all these years, I still like coming through there, that 90-mile section of trail. It is said that the real race for the finish begins after Unalakleet, which is nearly 300 miles from Nome.

After Unalakleet, we were still going good. I had fifteen dogs left, and my leader, Ruby, led us to Nome. When I got to the finish I cried. I couldn't believe we were there. I was just awestruck at the ability of the dogs, what they had done and what they had come through. They were amazing. There was such a feeling of sharing all that time with the dogs, of working together to reach a goal.

I had finished in 17 days, 7 hours, 59 minutes, placing twenty-fourth out of thirty-six finishers. The winner, Joe May, finished exactly three days ahead of me. My mother and Mike were there and I felt really proud. They said nice things about being proud of me, too.

I also felt humbled by the obstacles we had overcome and the vast country we saw. I'm always thankful to the Lord for all the opportunities I get, and I was thankful I had the chance to race the Iditarod and reach the finish. It was a tremendous feeling of coming to the end of a journey. You feel pretty special after doing something like that. You feel whatever happens, it's okay, because you've done it.

When you get to the finish line, you're tired and elated and you have trouble thinking clearly until you catch up on your sleep. Before the race I felt it would be the only Iditarod I would ever do, but within a month I changed my mind. It was such a great experience that I had to do it again.

This was my competitive side coming out. I knew I could race the Iditarod in a more efficient manner, that I was capable of getting better and finishing higher. I certainly had a lot of room for improvement.

It's the same in every sport. When you're just starting out, there are gigantic improvements. But when you get to the top level, the improvements become more gradual.

The difference between me as a racer in 1980 and me as a racer now is monumental. The first time I just wanted to get to Nome. Now I want to get to Nome fast.

And first.

I start training pups when they're six months old.

CHAPTER 7

BUILDING THE TEAM

I did an interview several years ago where I said that I had been a Girl Scout, and that when I was on the trail I ran my dog team as if it was a Girl Scout troop. I said that we have weenie roasts and give merit badges, while some other teams are like the Marine Corps and have forced marches.

As soon as I got home from the 1993 Iditarod, I evaluated every dog. I brought them in the house one by one, took a close look at them, and treated the little aches that any competitor gets by running a marathon. Then we took eight-mile runs, little happy runs. I like my Girl Scouts to feel good. It was a quiet recuperation time.

The weeks after the Iditarod involve a deceleration for the dogs who raced more than a thousand miles. They are used to training hard every day and building up to the big event, so once it's over you want to taper them down. I call it "de-training." We take the dogs out on the trails only a few days a week.

That way they come down from the peak level of fitness in a gradual, reasonable manner. They work out any stiffness from racing. It's better than just sitting around. I liken it to the way my knee feels if I just sit for days on end. It feels better when I move than when I sit.

April is also the time when the youngest puppies get broken in to harnesses. Nine puppies, just six months old, got their first taste of mushing by wearing a harness on short runs. I usually took them out in the early morning, because in the spring the snow gets mushy from the stronger sun later in the afternoon. Our trails behind the house in the woods were good and hard, and they stayed that way for a while.

Building an Iditarod team is a perpetual, year-round process. You're always looking to improve the team. In that way, it's just like a professional basketball team or football team. Even if a team wins the championship or the Super Bowl, the team doesn't stay the same. Some players retire, get traded, are past their prime.

With some puppies, you can sense right away that they are athletes. They just naturally want to run. It's amazing. These are little guys, far from fully grown, so they only run a mile and a half. We even stop during that short run. I encourage them, pat them. It's all fun.

But some puppies get spooked by the whole experience of trying to run with other dogs. When I find that in a dog, I take the puppy out of the mix, put it in a harness, and let it pull a car tire with no rim. The tire is lightweight, but simulates the motion of pulling a sled.

One of the puppies, Poncho, had this problem. I took him for walks one-on-one with his harness on, and I had him pull a tire for about ten minutes every other day. After a week, I hooked him into a six-dog team, and he took right to it. That was the end of any nervousness he had about the situation. Nerves is usually all it is.

Even when it is only six months old, you can tell things about a husky that will help you decide its racing future. Right away, Mike and I could see that two of the puppies, Job and Ruth, didn't mind running up front in the team. They were comfortable trying new things. That's a good sign. It doesn't necessarily mean they will become leaders, but it does mean they have a good chance if you help them along.

You have to work to develop leaders. You can make a mistake and discourage a dog's natural energy and spirit by doing something like putting it in lead on an icy trail. Or by putting it in lead in front of too large a team. You don't want to push the dog too far, too fast.

Out of any group of puppies, it's hard to predict just how many will eventually make the Iditarod team, much less become leaders. I like to think the odds are in my favor because of my carefully planned breeding program.

The parents of my dogs are not matched by accident. You can plan what kind of litter you will get — with endurance traits or speed traits — by researching what kind of pups the parents throw. You want to match bloodlines to help the process along in a scientific way.

However, you can't be sure what traits a pup will have. You try to figure it out the best you can before you start, but just as there are no guarantees that your baby will look like you, there are no guarantees a planned dog birth will result in an animal with the perfect blend of speed and stamina to be an Iditarod star. Genetics is not that exact a science. We are not cloning dogs.

The thing I'm driving for, with a lot of research and care through a planned breeding, is the likelihood of a high rate of success. By the time this group of puppies came along, I had been running a breeding program for six years. The secret is doing a lot of homework prior to breeding. You hope that you will get everything that was wonderful from both of the parents' bloodlines.

The idea is not to mass-produce puppies and hope for the best. I don't want a huge group of puppies running around. If you have a lot of puppies at once, your emotional commitment to each puppy is reduced so that puppy isn't getting the amount of love it needs. You are shortchanging each puppy. By breeding indiscriminately, you are shortchanging your whole program.

My life as a dog musher is complicated because I am developing two teams at once. Every January, I participate in the Alpirod, which is nearly 600 miles long but is a series of sprints. And I also compete in the Iditarod every March. So I'm recruiting for two different types of teams.

For 1994, I had thirteen new dogs at rookie level, who had the chance to move into the twenty-dog Iditarod team. But I also had twenty-three veterans. In the fall, thirty-six dogs would be in training for the 1994 Iditarod. It was going to take more than six months — right up until race day — for me to pick the twenty I wanted to take to Nome.

For the 1994 Alpirod, my goal was to field a thirteen-dog team, and I had eleven veterans in top form after the 1993 race. I also had some young dogs which had been on loan to other mushers, and some of them would be ready. But I feel I need to have twenty starting the season to have thirteen to race, so clearly I was going to do a bit more recruitment.

That spring I did three new breedings, the first on March 24. I matched Martina, who ran the 1993 Alpirod, with Taurus, who comes out of world champion sprint musher Roxy Wright Champaine's kennel. Taurus had run the Alpirod, too, and he's got lots of confidence.

On April 21, I bred Elroy, who did so terrifically for me in the Alpirod and the Iditarod, with Hillary. I hoped their litter would consist of dogs able to run in either race. I have been trying to do that more and more — have dogs that can go either way, not be specialized stock.

It used to be clear that the big, strong, muscular, heavy dogs were for the Iditarod and the thinner, leaner dogs were for sprint racing. But it's kind of blended over the years. Iditarod dogs have shrunk. You don't see those gigantic malemute-type 70- or 80-pounders in the Iditarod anymore. Sprint dogs and long-distance dogs have become more alike and somewhat interchangeable. I'm after a more speed-oriented, tough dog that I could take on the Alpirod or the Iditarod. I don't think the races are mutually exclusive. Elroy proved that in 1993. On April 22, I also bred Elroy to Whitney, Hillary's half-sister.

My breeding program may sound pretty rigid, but you don't get to that point without a lot of trial and error done over a lot of years.

After my first Iditarod in 1980, I tried again in 1981 and I did not have a good race. Instead of improving I fell back to thirty-first place. So I took 1982 off and returned to the race in 1983. I spent the year training and talking to other mushers, and I was pleased to make a move up to fifteenth place. In 1984, though, I dropped back down to thirtieth place and I realized I had to do something differently.

I began my own breeding program with the goal of breaking into the top echelon of mushers with all of my own dogs. I wanted to challenge at the front, to be top-ten, and I felt that was the best way to do it. That was a turning point.

It meant building a team almost from scratch. I investigated what kind of dogs were equipped to run. I asked a lot of questions. I studied the history of the race. I examined bloodlines. There were people who had been at it for years and years, and they had developed a certain type of dog which helped them win or place high in the standings.

There is no one successful kind of dog. They are all huskies, but with variations. If only one kind of dog, bred in a specific way, could win the Iditarod, then Susan Butcher would win every single year. But that isn't the case. Martin Buser, who won the race for the first time in 1992, has a whole different bloodline. The same is true in sprint mushing. Roxy Wright Champaine wins world championships with different types of dogs than ten-time world champion George Attla. There are many successful lines out there. The key is to match what you want from the dogs with your own personality.

In 1984, I decided I was in the sport of long-distance mushing for the long run. I had to fall back and build a new team that first and foremost would respond to me. I had to consider what I wanted and weigh what I had seen in different dogs.

I guess because of my own personality, I wanted friendly dogs which liked to be handled and needed some nurturing. I wanted good feet; I had spent too much time on my hands and knees putting booties on dogs. I wanted to see an eager attitude, not a dog that just stood in one place. And since I was living in Bethel at the time, I needed dogs with good coats that could weather the cold. I was also looking for a fast trotter with a smooth gait.

That's how I ended up with some Sue Firmin dogs. They were fast dogs, but also dogs that were a little bit high-strung. They needed more feeding. They were not your tough village dogs you could just throw a fish to. You had to spend time with them, but I felt they were worth it. This was a line of dogs I liked and I felt I could develop. I built my team from that line. In the 1993 Iditarod, ten of the twenty dogs on my team had come from the Sue Firmin bloodline.

Many of my early dogs weighed around 35 pounds and I decided that wasn't right. And some were around 70 pounds, and that wasn't right, either. So I decided my perfect weight would be dogs which weighed about 50 pounds.

All of that combined into the profile of a DeeDee Jonrowe dog, and I began working to develop my perfect Iditarod racing dog.

While I was trying to build a new team, I did not enter either the 1985 or 1986 Iditarod. I made my comeback in 1987. I had high hopes for my performance, but things didn't go as planned, and I finished in twenty-second place.

That did not make me happy. Susan Butcher asked me, "What happened?" and I didn't really know. That year the pace was fast and I thought I had a top-twenty team for sure.

Maybe I was just too

> "IN 1988, I HAD MY BREAKTHROUGH RACE. I FINISHED NINTH, MY FIRST TIME IN THE TOP TEN, AND I'VE BEEN IN THE TOP TEN EVERY YEAR SINCE."

impatient. That was when I got Johnnie, a silver and white dog who was really special to me. I just fell in love with him. It was his mind, his desire to please you, that set him apart. He was bow-legged, with a big front end and a big head, and those things should have hindered his speed. But he just had a desire to give every challenge more. He also had wonderful endurance, and was incredibly powerful.

The 1987 race taught me that Johnnie wasn't enough — I needed more good dogs. The dogs I had were good, but I didn't have enough of them. I went to Susan, and she helped me out. I got a couple of dogs from her.

In 1988, I had my breakthrough race. I finished ninth, my first time in the top ten, and I've been in the top ten every year since.

You're always learning. Improvement comes slowly and sometimes there are setbacks. In 1989, I challenged for first place for the first time. Traveling at the front of the pack was a different world. I was with all the best-known, most skilled mushers.

It was a fast pace — as it almost always seems to be now, weather permitting — and as we approached Nome, coming in from Safety, just 22 miles from the finish, I had third place sewn up. Joe Runyan of Nenana won the 1989 race in 11 days, 5 hours, 24 minutes and Susan finished second, just about an hour behind him.

I thought I was a lock for third. Instead, I had one of the most celebrated non-finishes any musher ever had. We were on the outskirts of Nome, four miles from the finish, and the dogs wouldn't go. They lay down, sort of went on strike. While I was sitting there, camped by the side of the trail, Rick Swenson passed me for third.

The fact that the dogs stopped was my fault. It was mental overload. Physically, the dogs were fine. But I had asked too much of them. I had pushed too hard on the 55-mile stretch from White Mountain to Safety. I was urging the dogs on, exhorting them, all the time. I think I put too much pressure on them to finish, and they were telling me they wanted to take some time off.

Also, it was a sunny late afternoon, and hundreds of spectators had driven out of town along the trail to watch the mushers finish. Because there was a crowd all around, the atmosphere made it seem like we were at the finish. The dogs figured they were there, all done. I blame myself. I don't blame the dogs. The dogs will only respond when you've trained them properly. I was furious at myself, then and for months later.

I felt humiliated. The end was in sight, and I couldn't get there. I was stuck and the whole world knew it. I was not in an isolated area. I was right out there in front of everybody. The TV cameras were right on us.

The dogs' rebellion lasted six hours. I just had to wait it out, let them rest, and stay by the sled until the dogs told me they were willing to run again. I ended up finishing about 11 p.m., but I got a nice reception from the fans anyway. I think they had some sympathy for me.

Every year people come up to me and tell me I've got to win. But they don't really understand what you're up against out on the trail: the elements, the competition, the terrain. You can only do your best, but it's not easy. The dogs deserve for you to do your best, but what is your best? I guess my best was fourth place that year.

Dogs and mushers work together to get through bad weather and other dangers.

CHAPTER 8

THROUGH THE STORM TOGETHER

One of the greatest challenges a musher can face in the Iditarod is meeting an Alaskan winter head-on.

Weather on the Iditarod Trail is often dangerous, especially on the Bering Sea Coast when the winds roar in and buffet you. The temperature is well below zero and the windchill factor can be 100 below.

Many times, when you get caught in a storm like that, you circle the wagons. You just pull off the trail, let the dogs burrow into the snow, and you zip yourself into the sled bag. Other times, when you get caught unawares, it's best to keep traveling because you're closing in on a village.

The most peculiar situation is a ground blizzard. Above you the sky might be blue, but the snow around you is whipped into an impenetrable swirl, obliterating visibility. It's like mushing in a milk jug. Everything's white. There is no density, no depth perception.

The worst ground blizzard I ever faced was not on the Iditarod Trail. I was out on a training run near Bethel in 1986, with an inexperienced friend along for company. We were going out for a three-hour ride when we got whomped by the weather.

You couldn't see the terrain. You couldn't see the top of any mountain or the bottom of any valley. You couldn't see the end of the dog team from the sled runners. It was terrible. We had to stop and wait it out. We had no matches, no food, and no water. I hadn't brought any because we were only going out for the afternoon. I didn't even have my warmest boots on. It was the all-time scare of my life.

We were stuck for three days. Hypothermia was setting in. We just waited out the storm, though, and mushed ourselves home. It was scary, but we outlasted the weather and got home in one piece.

I grew up a lot on that trip. I learned that you should be prepared for anything, even on a short training run. You don't forget a situation like that. I was very scared when it was happening, but once it was over, I gained confidence, because I realized there was a way through the situation. I think I also gained faith. My faith in God has grown stronger every time I've taken it to the edge. You can either handle it or fall completely apart. But you can't afford to fall apart, so you pull yourself together and fall apart later.

During the 1991 Iditarod, I was leaving the village of Shaktoolik when I got whacked by a vicious storm. The wind was howling. I wanted to stop, but there was no place that offered any kind of shelter at all. We were on the sea ice, totally vulnerable. I was afraid if I stopped the dogs would not start again. I didn't want them lying down on the ice. We mushed along very slowly, the wind blasting us, pushing us sideways. My right cheek got frostbitten and my nose got frost-nipped.

When I first started mushing and got trapped by my first big storm in the Kuskokwim 300, I had been inexperienced. But by the time I got ensnared in this storm, I had eleven years of mushing background. Experience makes the difference. You think,

"Well, I've been through this before."

You don't panic. You know your dogs and have faith in them. I knew I could get through the storm then. Rather than being scared, I just viewed the storm as an obstacle preventing me from going from here to there.

Dogs and mushers work as partners to get through the storm. You let your lead dogs sniff out the trail, finding the wooden stakes with orange ribbons that serve as trail markers — if the markers haven't blown down. That's one way you can lose the trail altogether. The markers aren't planted in concrete, and a harsh wind can easily uproot them.

"MUSHERS ARE VERY COMPETITIVE, BUT SAFETY, HELPING ANOTHER MUSHER, ALWAYS TAKES PRECEDENCE. THAT'S PART OF THE CODE OF THE TRAIL."

There may be other mushers and teams around you in a tough fix, too. That's when mushers cooperate. We know that in a storm we can do better working together than we can singly. When mushers are traveling together in a bad storm, we trade off taking the lead and breaking trail. That's work if the trail is buried under fresh snow. The dogs push hard, so it's not fair for one team to lead all the time.

Mushers are very competitive, but safety, helping another musher, always takes precedence. That's part of the code of the trail. No victory is so important you allow dogs or mushers to remain in jeopardy if you can help them. Many times mushers have stopped their own races, hindered their own chances for prize money, to help out. In 1989, Mike Madden collapsed by the side of the trail, and a whole group of mushers, all of them fighting for top-twenty money and several of them for rookie-of-the-year honors, pulled over, built a fire, made him eat and drink, put him in sleeping bags and went for help. Mike had to be evacuated by small plane; it turned out he was suffering from salmonella poisoning.

Mushers occasionally lose their teams. You might be going along, dozing on the back of the sled, and all of a sudden you hit a huge bump. You fall off, and the dogs run ahead without you. It's happened to me. It happens to lots of people. But if a musher is coming along the trail behind you and sees you, even if he's a top rival, he isn't going to leave you. It's not safe for a musher to be wandering alone in the wilderness with no food or water. Likewise, any musher who sees a loose team will try to stop it and anchor it, even if it means tying it to a tree.

Terry Adkins needed help in 1992. It was 45 degrees below zero in the Farewell Burn, and he lost his team. He stopped to put another layer of clothing on and the dogs got away from him. I picked him up, of course. You'd have to be pretty cold-hearted to leave a person, or a dog, in trouble in the Alaska wilderness. I was not going to leave Terry walking around out there in the cold. I picked him up and we found his team a few miles later.

Not long after I dropped Terry, my team was charging along, really zooming. We came to a small pole bridge, but we were going so fast that the sled runners slipped sideways and we fell off the bridge into a creek bed. I went flying and hit the ground hard. I lost my grip on the sled handlebars, and with all my gloves and mittens I couldn't grasp them again quickly. The team was just gone. They had just dumped Terry and his 200 pounds. With me off too, the sled was more than 300 pounds lighter, and they were happy.

My first fear was that something would happen to the dogs. I wondered if I would ever see the dogs again, if they would be irretrievably lost, or if a dog would get killed from his own recklessness. I loved and cherished those dogs. I started praying, "Please don't let them be gone. Please let me find those dogs."

I started walking along the trail. After about ten minutes, Terry Adkins came along and picked me up. Rick Swenson passed Terry and asked what was going on. Rick was moving faster, and he invited me to ride with him. He didn't have to do that. I already had help, but he volunteered because he knew I'd be able to catch up to my dogs quicker.

Also, Rick is not going to let twenty dogs run free like that. Rick often comes off as being gruff, but he cares about his competitors and all the race dogs. I rode on the back of the sled with him while we looked for my dogs. It was about 45 minutes, several miles, before I got my dogs back. They were just sitting by the side of the trail, resting, waiting for DeeDee to rejoin them.

In 1990, I depended on the kindness of Tim Osmar over the final stretch of the race. We were fighting it out for fourth and fifth place when we reached White Mountain.

It was night and I needed more batteries for my headlamp, but the checkers couldn't find my supplies. Naturally, it was storming, too. Not a good situation to be in. Without batteries, the headlamp was useless. I could choose between having my race paralyzed at White Mountain or plunging into the dark with no way to see.

I tried, but I could not really go on. Pulling over by the side of the trail, I could see how badly the trail was drifted over. Each time we came to a drift, the dogs wanted to go around rather than through the snow, so they would get off the trail. I did not want to lose the trail. I could have ended up in Siberia.

I sat down to wait, either until the next musher came along — Tim was a half hour behind — or until I could see.

Tim came up behind me on the trail and stopped. We made a

deal. He said I could follow him and benefit from the use of his light if I promised not to pass him. It was a good deal for me because I needed the help. And it was a good deal for Tim because he didn't have to worry about me beating him.

Tim was very gracious. He could have just mushed on past with the light, and I couldn't have followed in the dark. I could have tried to follow him without making a deal, but that never would have worked for very long. He trusted that I would hold up my part of the bargain, and I appreciated his gesture. A couple of times, he even turned back and shined his light on the snow for me and pointed to where my lead dogs were supposed to go.

Without his cooperation I couldn't have got to Nome as quickly. Tim's official finish time was 11 days, 14 hours, 40 minutes, 53 seconds in fourth place, and I was timed in 38 seconds behind him. The difference in prize money was between $20,000 and $15,000, but what can you do? It wouldn't have been that close if he hadn't helped me.

Another great hazard of the Iditarod is moose. Most people think of moose as friendly, gangly animals who don't give anyone any trouble. Those people don't live in Alaska. Each year there are hundreds of collisions between moose and cars on the highways outside of Anchorage. Vehicles are dented or demolished, and many moose are killed.

In the wilderness, a different type of collision occurs. In 1985, Susan Butcher thought she had her best dog team ever, but it was attacked by a moose. Dogs are moose magnets, I guess. They bark and jump around, and the moose get irritated. A single, 1,200-pound moose can create havoc with its hooves if it is in a bad mood. There is no telling how much damage that moose would have done if musher Dewey Halverson hadn't come along and shot it. As it was, dogs were injured and killed, and Susan had to drop out of the race.

I carry a .38-caliber pistol with me in the sled for protection. Of course, if your lead dogs are going around a corner, they're so far in front of you that you can't even see them, and a lot can happen swiftly if you surprise a moose. I've never shot anything on the trail. I have run up on a moose and shot the gun in the air to scare it away. It worked. I also carry firecrackers. I think they work better. I don't want to kill a moose, but you have to be prepared.

You try to think of anything that can possibly happen, to be prepared for anything, but you can't really, because the Iditarod is an unpredictable race. No matter how smart and ready you are, you never know when the storm is coming. And a storm always comes. There are always surprises in the Iditarod.

I try to create the right atmosphere for training championship dogs.

CHAPTER 9

AT HOME IN THE KENNELS

All winter, a layer of snow covers my backyard. I can look out my kitchen window and see the dogs and their little wooden box houses. They can duck in and out the doorways at will. Their chains are just long enough to prevent them from getting tangled with each other. Sometimes so much snow falls that the houses are buried up to the roofs. Mike and I get help from handlers shoveling the yard. That can be pretty time-consuming after a storm.

After the Iditarod, by the end of April, the ground is thawed and most of the snow is melted. Winter has left its mark, and Mike and I do a major cleanup.

A couple of weeks after I got home from the 1993 Iditarod — in between all of my appearances — we took all of the dog houses out of the remaining ice and removed all of the old straw bedding. We dried the houses, raked up the pieces of old straw, then lay down new bedding.

We have experimented with different ways to keep the kennel

as dry as possible — using gravel bases, removing the straw to let the ground dry faster. Sometimes it is still a sea of mud.

We mount the dishes on the houses to keep them out of the dirt. It helps prevent food from spilling out into the gravel. I worry that a dog picking around for nuggets of food will lap up a rock. If the dog didn't pass it, the rock could cause quite a stomachache and even require surgery.

In feeding sled dogs, the idea is to obtain a high-caloric food with little volume. You want all of the nutrients packed in tightly. Volume is a limiting factor with dogs. They just will not eat huge quantities of food. I don't think dogs would do well at all-you-can-eat buffets.

In the summer, when it's warmer and the dogs aren't working as hard, I feed the dogs once a day. They get water twice a day. In the winter, when they're at the peak of their workout periods, running a lot of miles, they get fed three times a day, sometimes even four, depending on how cold it is. That's a time-consuming process. We snack them in the morning, snack them when they come in from a daily run, and feed them again at night. If we go out on a long run, we snack them during the run, too.

They're not gluttons, though, but more like people who eat a little bit at a sitting rather than really chowing down. I feel that dogs do better when they maintain a stable blood sugar by eating steadily, rather than going long periods without sustenance.

Frequent feeding year-round parallels the feeding on the Iditarod Trail, too. We try to keep the dogs well-fed when they are racing, to keep them on an even keel. You never want the dogs to get down during the Iditarod. If you let them get too short of rations and try to build them back up, it's just not going to happen. They never recoup. You have to keep them stable all the way through the race.

I also try to give my dogs as much water as possible. But I feed my dogs dry food rather than soggy, soaked food. Some mushers take chunks of dry food and wet them down, claiming that this way they are giving their dogs more water. But I don't think it's the way to go.

Two things are happening when a dog is being given sopping wet food. Yes, they are getting more water, but water has a faster transit time in the intestine than solid food, so food is washed through the intestine too fast. That means the dogs are not getting as much opportunity to absorb the nutrients that are in the food.

"YOU LEARN EVERYTHING THROUGH EXPERIMENTATION, THROUGH TRIAL AND ERROR."

Plus, as soon as you put water on that food, you begin the digestive process. You are taking away from the integrity of the nutritional value of that food by adding moisture to it. And if you let it sit too long in the dish, in the open, you've got the bacteria count going up. That's the advantage of dry food over a lot of meat products. Dry food isn't going to sour on you or get moldy, but all that changes once you put water on it.

I tried feeding my dogs different ways, but this is the way I found works best. You learn everything through experimentation, through trial and error.

After the post-Iditarod deceleration and the melting of snow, the dogs are on vacation for a while. The trails are muddy and soft and messy. Running through the mud would furrow the trails, creating ruts and indentations that would stay for a long time. After the trails dry, I start running the dogs again. Just short maintenance

LEW FREEDMAN

Dinnertime in the dog yard always means a lot of excitement.

runs through the spring, a couple of days a week.

Comparatively few Iditarod fans realize that when the snow is gone, we still mush. Instead of a toboggan sled skimming over the snow, the driver rides an all-terrain vehicle. My dogs pull a Honda four-wheeler with a modified brake system and grips. It has to have a good suspension system so I'm not being thrashed around. Having a comfortable machine is important because it takes some of the stress off my elbows and my back. It prevents me from wearing down.

We call this period of riding on dry land "cart training." It gives the dogs something to do. In all, I have nearly a hundred dogs in my kennel. Technically, you could say I have two dog lots since the yards are split between two areas on our property. One group of dogs is right next to the house. That's where my wire-mesh pens for the pups are, too. The second lot is in a clearing through the birch trees about a hundred yards from the front door.

I have Iditarod dogs and the contenders for that team. I have Alpirod dogs and contenders for that team. I've got puppies just getting started and some retired dogs from my old teams who are just good old pets these days, dogs who helped me and raced for me, like Johnnie, Goldie, Jade, Atlas. Except for Johnnie, they are all into double-figure ages, eleven or so. In dog years that's about seventy-seven, so you can see why they are no longer racing.

Johnnie, my great leader, has an exalted place in the kennel. I wish he could be factored into my breeding system, but when he retired at age nine in 1993, it was because of an abcessed prostrate, so we had to neuter him. Now he usually gets turned loose for five or six hours a day with the older dogs, like Goldie and Jade, just to play in the yard and frolic in the woods.

I estimate it costs $100,000 a year to operate my kennel. Even if I won the $50,000 first prize in the Iditarod — and I earned $43,000 for second in 1993 — that alone wouldn't support my kennel.

Still, I don't raise dogs to sell dogs. When I do sell one, it's more important to me to find a good home and situation for the dog than to wring the maximum amount of money from someone. Good sled dogs go for several hundred dollars apiece now, and leaders can cost thousands of dollars. You are buying the reputation of the kennel, the musher, and the pedigree. Some mushers do sell dogs specifically to help support the kennel costs, but that's not my aim. If I was just trying to produce dogs, I would have a lot more than nine puppies in a year.

A lot of work goes into establishing a kennel, a lot of behind-the-scenes tasks and chores which create the proper atmosphere for training championship-quality dogs. There are so many chores to do to keep the yard presentable. Mike and I try to put in some kind of capital improvement each year, and we're pretty much the construction team.

The big project for 1992 was building a handler's cabin, a place for a live-in handler to stay. For 1993 it was putting cement floors in my puppy pens. I wanted the floors to be smooth enough that I could keep them clean all the time, bleaching them with Clorox. It is a healthier environment when everything is disinfected. Like babies, puppies are susceptible to catching all kinds of bugs and viruses, and I wanted to minimize the chances of illness.

Building a top sled dog team is a year-round proposition. When you're not actually out on the trail mushing, you're getting ready to mush. That might involve driving nails, cradling a sick puppy, or shoveling dog poop. We definitely shovel a lot. We pick up the yard twice a day.

I once heard of a book by a man who operated a thoroughbred horse racetrack. He called his book *Thirty Tons a Day*. I know exactly what he's talking about. I don't know the sheer amount of waste products created by nearly a hundred dogs, but I can identify with that guy.

You can't be squeamish, that's for sure. And picking up after your dogs just comes with the territory. The reward comes when you are mushing alone across the smooth trail on a silent night with the colors of the northern lights shimmering in the sky.

You never waste your time by snuggling an armful of puppies.

CHAPTER 10
HAPPY BIRTH DAYS

For some reason, puppies are never born during the day. You can count on being up all night when dogs are due. It's like always getting a rainy day when you plan a picnic.

One of the craziest nights of my mushing life occurred in late June. I got home at midnight and the dogs were barking, barking, barking. I was thinking how unusual it was, and how I would really like them to be quiet so the neighbors wouldn't complain. I didn't think they needed a late-night symphony. My closest neighbor is about a quarter of a mile away, but the sound really travels in Willow at night. There's no other noise at all.

My first guess was that a dog was loose and running around the yard. I checked. Nope. That wasn't it. It turned out that two of my dogs, Whitney and Hillary, were giving birth on the same night. All the dogs in the yard were following these events, so they were yipping and excited.

By the time I had wandered through the yard, Whitney had already had a couple of puppies. They popped out one by one all night long, from about 1 a.m. to 6 a.m., squealing and squeaking. Hillary had six puppies, five males and a female. Whitney had three females and two males. Eleven in one night!

I watched the whole thing to make sure nothing went wrong. Sometimes a pup will be stillborn, but for the most part the dogs don't have any trouble birthing. This time all the puppies were healthy.

Both of the moms had been bred to Elroy, a great dog and a veteran of both the Iditarod and Alpirod. I was real interested to see how the puppies would develop, but I wouldn't know for a couple of years. Some of these dogs wouldn't fully mature until they were three or even four years old. Still, I was hopeful some good dogs would come out of those groups to become members of the Iditarod team.

A month earlier, I had four puppies born, giving me fifteen for the season. Martina, named for the tennis player Martina Navratilova, was the mother. I also had bred Elroy to one of Sue Firmin's dogs and we split the litter. That gave me two more pups. By breeding Elroy to three different bloodlines, I had the opportunity to see the genetic components he could contribute without having a massive number of puppies.

I love raising puppies. They bunch up, jump on one another, cuddle each other. You can pick up several of them in your arms at once and hug them. That first two weeks after they are born is a time when you can really bond. Their eyes aren't even open yet

From the very beginning, I try to introduce newborn puppies to human beings and give them a lot of love. A couple of teenage girls who live next door come over and like to play with the puppies. I urge the girls to take the puppies for walks and pet them. I want the puppies to be snuggled and cuddled. They need a lot of attention. In their first weeks of life, the puppies are shy. Some are born shy and stay that way. Others get used to people quickly.

Martina was very shy as a puppy. You couldn't put your hands on her. The first time I got near her, she wanted to bite me.

She grew up, and now she's just a big friendly baby to everyone. You can develop that friendliness.

It's best to recognize an innate shyness right away, though, and work it out. Sometimes, puppies will just dash right under the dog pen when you're coming. That's a clue for me. Or a pup acts as if it is being punished when you pick it up. Another reason it's good to kill that shyness off right away is that the puppies are so young they can't run away from you. If you play with them, talk nice to them, and stroke them, it helps a lot.

"FROM THE BEGINNING, I TRY TO INTRODUCE NEWBORN PUPPIES TO HUMAN BEINGS AND GIVE THEM A LOT OF LOVE."

It's fun to watch puppies grow out of it. It's a pleasure when they get to the point where they don't shrink away from your hand when you pet them. After they're no longer scared, the next step in their development is coaxing them away from their little buddies and their mom and taking them for walks in the woods.

When they are about a month old, I start taking the pups for walks with my Labrador retrievers. I have three Labs who are house dogs — Widgeon Maru, Teal Star, and Remington — but they also help with the husky training by being role models. The Labradors are very well behaved and they do not stray far from me when we take walks, so they set a good example. Unlike sled dogs. Those huskies just zip down the trail. Whenever I say, "Come," though, the Labs come back. The puppies follow the Labradors, so they come back too. The Labradors are like aunts and uncles to them.

For their first four months, I keep my puppies segregated in their own pens in a corner of the dog yard. The pens are big, as big as the living room in my house, so they have lots of room to roam. They gather at feeding time and play together.

It's important to keep them in a sterile environment until they've been through the vaccination program to protect them. At an early age, puppies are vulnerable. They can be exposed to a virus or to parvo, an illness that attacks the intestinal system and strips away the lining. Adult dogs are usually carriers, but they are strong enough to withstand the disease. Puppies' immune systems aren't developed enough to protect them. Dogs with parvo get incredibly sick. We had nine pups in 1992, and they got it and one of them died. For this reason, puppies are kept away from the adult team.

After four months, the puppies are put on a chain with their own house, their own food dish, just like the big dogs. When the dogs are first put on a chain, they tend to throw a temper-tantrum. It might last for two hours, or even twelve hours, but they get used to it. But when they figure out they've got this house for themselves, they really like that.

In a few more months, their bodies have developed, their legs have gained strength, and they are used to being on the chain. They've learned how to eat when food is presented to them. They've taken all those walks and they're used to your voice: they have bonded with you.

The next step in the puppies' evolution is to start harness-breaking them. A lot of times, puppies will just go, just run, as soon as they get put in harness. They get excited because they've been watching the adults run and they think it's the cat's meow. They think it's really cool that it's their turn.

Once in a while, of course, a young dog will be spooked by the experience of having a harness on its body and rebel. That dog has to be taken out alone. All that early petting and soothing talk is critical. If you haven't bonded with a dog by the time it is four months old, you probably won't. You won't be able to alter a lot of personality traits after that age.

Human contact at a young age is just really important. It doesn't have to be me doing all the handling. My grandmother visited from Virginia in 1992, and she loves puppies. She sat with a lap full of puppies for hours at a time, snuggling them.

The puppies bring out a sentimental side in me, too. Mike and I don't have any children, and the puppies are like having youngsters added to the family. I love playing with them. You always wish you could freeze them in time, so they would always be little bitty puppies playing with you. That has nothing to do with racing. That's just enjoying being around little animals.

I snuggle with them all the time. You can never waste time by sitting still and cuddling a puppy. That time comes back to you later in affection from the dog and its willingness to run for you. They just grow up into big friends. The fruits of all the years of snuggling come out in my top-ten finishes with big teams in the Iditarod.

I know mushers love their dogs and treat them with the best possible care.

CHAPTER 11

INTO THE ARENA

My foray into politics began when I was elected to the Iditarod Trail Committee's board of directors as the mushers' representative. The one-year term started in June 1993, and it put me into the middle of the administration of the race I love.

It was my desire to bring an uncolored, unprejudiced view to the board about what mushers feel. I didn't have a personal agenda. I just felt the Iditarod was facing a critical time with animal rights groups, and I was willing to work hard and take on the role of representing drivers.

In recent years, the race has been under attack from critics who suggest that mushers don't take good care of their dogs and don't care about their dogs' health. The Humane Society of the United States has injected itself into the race and issued many criticisms of our behavior — most of which we consider to be totally unfair.

I was getting a little angry with the animal rights groups. We mushers refuse to accept the idea that we are cruel and inhumane people. We are not! I'm sure that the average Iditarod dog gets better care than 99 percent of the dogs in America.

The Humane Society tries to make mushers out to be puppy-killers. The truth is that we use well-thought-out, premeditated breeding programs. We aren't producing puppies indiscriminately.

The Humane Society also tries to portray us as forcing the animals to run against their will. Well, the dogs love to run. If anyone has ever seen huskies on the starting line of a race, they would be amazed at how badly the dogs want to run. They're straining at the harnasses, anxious to go!

Iditarod dogs are fed the best food — food that is high in protein, rich in nutrients, and quite expensive. Unlike dogs who are pets in the city, these dogs aren't cooped up in an apartment all day, waiting for an owner to come home from work. They get regular feedings each day and regular exercise. As far as I'm concerned, my dogs are members of the family.

I wanted to help get these points across to the public. As a member of the Iditarod Trail Committee, I was willing to work with animal rights groups to a point, but not to surrender control of the race. I was not going to just fall over dead and say, "Okay, just tell us what to do. What's acceptable to you?"

This is not their race. It belongs to the people of Alaska, to the long-time fans of dog mushing, and to the long-time volunteers and workers who make the Iditarod a great race. It is often said that Alaskans don't care how people do things in the Lower 48. There is some truth to that. There is a limit to how much guff Alaskans will take and how far they will let themselves be pushed by outsiders who feel they know more than we do about our lifestyles.

As a result of accusations by groups like the Humane Society, our relationship with sponsors has been affected. Some of our main sponsors have backed off from Iditarod involvement. In many ways, we feel we have been unjustly verbally assaulted, and that we have been put in the untenable position of defending ourselves against charges that are just untrue.

Mushers are great individualists. We don't all play on the same team like other professional athletes. We live in far-flung areas of the largest state in the union, and we don't often even see one another. In that sense, we are very vulnerable when someone disparages our sport, because we don't have a union or a truly organized voice to make a statement or to fight back.

Except for a few key positions, the Iditarod is primarily a volunteer-run organization. Being part of the board was very time-consuming. The meetings, in either Wasilla or Anchorage, only took place every month or so, but we had board meetings by phone also. And as I was the mushers' rep, a lot of mushers contacted me at home with their thoughts.

It was a time commitment, but I thought of my time on the board as giving something back to the race. Somebody has got to be willing to take on the responsibility and pursue it. You can't count on the same people doing all the work, all the time. Everybody needs to step up and take a turn. There has been a lot of pressure on board members for the last couple of years, as they have tried to appease the Humane Society and work with them. It's being on the hot seat, but it's not fair to expect just a few people to carry the burden.

After my election, the board faced these challenges. We spent

> "WE HAVE TO SHOW PEOPLE THAT WE LOVE OUR DOGS LIKE FAMILY, THAT WE CARE ABOUT OUR ATHLETES, AND THAT WE AREN'T BAD PEOPLE."

months negotiating new sponsor contracts with big Lower 48 companies. We put out an appeal for Alaskans to support the race more than ever by buying individual or family memberships. We also asked businesses around the state to step forward and become sponsors so we wouldn't have to rely on money from Outside companies. Those approaches worked very well. Our membership list jumped from about 800 to more than 2,000, and several large Alaska businesses did come through.

But I still think that one of the most important things we can do is to get our message across through education. We have to use any opportunity we have to let our public know what kind of people we really are. We have to show people that we love our dogs like family, that we care about our athletes, and that we aren't bad people.

Clearly, my opportunities to make public appearances increased markedly after I placed second in the 1993 Iditarod. And I used those opportunities. I took every chance I got to explain the joys and thrills of dog mushing. When I traveled and visited with people, often taking Johnnie with me, people had a million questions. Almost all of the questions were about the dogs and how I can stand the cold on the trail. When people meet me, they seem pretty excited. To them the Iditarod is something very romantic and adventurous. That's the image we want to perpetuate.

People don't accuse me of being cruel to dogs. To them, I think it's all a non-issue. The Humane Society has tried to make it into a big controversy, to convince corporations that they will draw the ire of their customers if they support the Iditarod, but I don't think the average person on the street really cares or knows what they're talking about.

The more people who meet us in the flesh — who take dog tours with our teams, who get the chance to ask us questions, who pet our dogs, who visit our kennels — the better off we all will be and the better off the Iditarod will be. Public relations is a key part of the entire debate. We have to be good public relations spokesmen and spokeswomen for our sport.

That's our responsibility, our challenge in the present and in the future. We all have to give something back to the Iditarod if we want it to continue to grow, expand, and remain such an important event on the Alaska winter scene.

As a guide, I helped sport fishermen catch prized king salmon.

CHAPTER 12

A SUMMER ON THE RIVER

During the summer of 1993, I was the cowgirl of the Talkeetna River. For years, I spent a large portion of my summer traveling to Bristol Bay for commercial fishing. But my new job was working as a sport fishing guide for Mahay's Riverboat Service of Talkeetna.

My guiding career started in May. I ran one charter boat a day, sometimes for fourteen days straight without a day off. A typical shift might be 4 to 9 p.m. But that's just time spent on the water. It's about a 35-mile drive each way from my house to the guide service offices in Talkeetna, and I had to spend some time setting up the boat for the clients when I got there. For a 4 p.m. dock departure, I had to leave home at 2 p.m.

The first thing I did each day was prepare the boat by loading the fishing rods and the bait. I also checked with guides who had gone out in the morning, asking them where the fish were biting. Where did they do well? Where did they think the fish were now? What were the water conditions? What kind of lures would be most effective?

That's before the clients ever got on board. On a given day, there

I loved driving my sturdy, aluminum-hulled fishing boat up and down the river.

were as many as six clients on a trip. We got all kinds of people on the boats. Fathers and sons. Single women. Tourists. Locals. Friends.

The boat I drove — and it has a steering wheel just like a car — is 27 feet long with high sides and an aluminum hull. It's a very sturdy machine, and it has to be. The river has a swift current, and the wakes thrown up will toss a smaller boat, or even swamp one that has low sides.

I loved driving the boat. At top speed, going from the dock to the fishing hole or back, I went about 35 miles per hour. You're really cutting through the water. There was a lot of traffic on the river in the middle of the summer, though, so I had to be careful. You can't just shut down in a hurry. You could plant the boat if you shut down too fast, because you're driving in about four inches of water.

It's several miles from the dock in Talkeetna to the best fishing spots. One place we went frequently was Clear Creek. The water doesn't quite dead-end in a cove there, but it's a cozy spot where you can pull in. Fishermen can either cast from the deck of the boat or climb off and fish from shore. Both ways work out pretty well.

When clients catch fish, the guide nets them and hauls them in. It was a lot more physical work than I expected. You do a lot of handling and hauling, so you stretch and strain the muscles in your arms and back plenty. It's a workout.

The fishermen are mainly after king salmon. The biggest king salmon are most commonly caught on Alaska's Kenai Peninsula. Each spring fish as large as 70, 80, or even 90 pounds are caught there. These fish are several feet long, as large as small children. The world record king salmon caught by a sport fisherman was taken in 1985 on the Kenai River: 97 and 1/4 pounds.

Typically, the king salmon that come farther north up the Talkeetna and Susitna Rivers are not nearly that big. But even a king salmon as small as 30 pounds is quite a fish — especially if you're used to fishing for five-pound lake fish in the continental United States.

King salmon are very coveted fish. They do not always aggressively take the bait, so they're harder to catch. And they're beautiful fish. Usually silvery, they give off a nice glow in afternoon sunlight. On these rivers, this far removed from the ocean, some have a reddish sheen. Obviously, since salmon is such a popular dish on restaurant menus, it's a very tasty fish. You can take them home and grill them, spreading some barbecue sauce or teriyaki sauce on them. Fishermen always say the best-tasting fish are the ones they catch themselves.

For me, dressing for success in king salmon guiding meant wearing hip waders over my jeans, a safari vest, and a black, wide-brimmed hat. Some people thought I was dressing a certain way for effect; someone even mentioned that my outfit resembled the one Arnold Schwarzenegger wore in *The Terminator*. I always used to think that those wide-brimmed hats were just part of the costume, but when I started working for Mahay's, Steve Mahay, the owner, told me to wear one all the time. There's a good reason for that. The wide brim keeps hooks out of your face.

Fishing hooks can be very dangerous weapons. They are sharp enough to catch and grip in a big fish's mouth, so you can imagine what kind of damage they are capable of doing if you get one in the eye. There are many stories about a hook being lodged in the cheek or neck of a careless fisherman. Emergency room workers at the hospital on the Kenai Peninsula keep a collection of the hooks they have removed from people's skin. So the hats may look cool, but they serve a practical purpose. In the first few weeks I was guiding, I had three or four hooks bounce off the rim of the hat. Steve's warning was right on target. No matter how warm it got, I wouldn't take that hat off.

Probably the single most frustrating thing was when I sincerely tried to help people catch fish and they didn't want to listen to me. I was out on the river every day. I was a professional. It was my job to know where the fish were. And yet there would be people who had never been there before, never even been to Alaska before, who thought they knew better.

I had fishermen constantly flinging out their bait — we use salmon roe, the tiny, round, bright red eggs taken from female fish — and it would just float on top of the water. That wasn't going to catch them fish. A fish would have to be airborne to bite it. I had to tell them in as a polite a fashion as possible, "Your lure is not in the water. You'll never catch a fish that way. You've got to leave it in the water." One of those fishermen who wouldn't listen nearly hooked my arm. I was lucky. He barely missed.

Being a guide is harder work than most people think, but it's

LEW FREEDMAN

One of my duties as a guide was preparing and loading the fishing rods and bait.

also really a wonderful job. Driving the boat up and down the river, gazing into the trees, or when we parked it while we were fishing, I got to see moose, eagles, and bears. It's a wildlife cornucopia.

People camp on Clear Creek, but it turned out humans weren't the only ones attracted to the salmon in that area. One night a grizzly bear swam across the river toward the tents. A dog one of the campers had brought started barking and woke everybody up. People shot over the bear's head, and it swam away.

This was a bear who figured out that fish make a good dinner and that this was a great fishing hole. He was just looking for fish, not trouble with people. In many instances, when a bear comes calling, the safest thing to do is just give him your cooler and walk away. You lose your fish, but you stay healthy. It's hard to win an argument with a bear.

We lost a lot of coolers there over the summer. After a while, I think that bear wised up and just came looking for fish-filled coolers. That's a bad sign for his future. Not every fisherman will be easygoing enough to relinquish his catch without a fight. Inevitably, there will be a confrontation between a human being with a gun who doesn't want to surrender his hard-earned salmon, and the bear who thinks that the best shopping is in a cooler. The bear will no longer be afraid of people, and someday somebody's going to get him for that.

I carried a twelve-gauge shotgun with me on the boat every day and kept it within reach any time we anchored the boat to fish. Bear behavior is unpredictable, so I didn't want to be without protection. It's bad form to lose a client to a prowling bear.

Besides bears, I saw eagles all the time. They are so majestic, the way they swoop through the sky and glide. At a different fishing hole, I saw a moose standing in a nearby slough. One day I saw a cow and a newborn calf. On clear days, you could see Mount McKinley, the tallest mountain in North America. It was an awesome sight, and I never got tired of it. The Talkeetna River is just a beautiful, beautiful place.

Every fishing trip, every day, was a different adventure. We started the day as strangers, but I tried to make sure those strangers, who might be fishing for king salmon for the only time in their lives, had a good time. Being a guide carries with it a lot more responsibility than just going out fishing for yourself. You have to be aware of the needs, the safety, and the happiness of everybody on board.

After we got in from fishing each night, we docked the boat, unloaded all the gear, then hauled the fish up the hill, through the trees, to the guide service office. We lined the fish up on hooks, took pictures, and weighed them. Then we carved them up into steak-sized pieces and bagged them so the clients could take the fish home. You can't be squeamish slicing up the fish with big, sharp knives.

The cutting area becomes a bloody mess, and your hands turn red and smell of fish.

After the clients and other guides left, I cured all the eggs taken from the female fish to be used as bait. I drained the fresh eggs, then put on them a chemical solution that's like raspberry jello. The color stays bright — that's more of an attractor. Then I added a brine that takes the moisture out. That makes the eggs stick together, so they won't break apart at the end of the hook when you throw them into the water.

By the time I finished curing the eggs, it was about 10:30 p.m. I got home about an hour later. I had a few marathons over the summer when I didn't get home to Willow until midnight and had to be back in Talkeetna at 5:30 a.m. the next day for a morning charter.

There were times during the summer when I was just as exhausted as I am in the winter during the height of dog training. All summer, I was always searching for time to go to the post office, or to make my house payment, or to do all the little things I had to get done. Sometimes I couldn't even find the time to go grocery shopping. Of course, it's not as if I have a grocery store right by my house. I have to drive to Wasilla to shop, and that's 60 miles round-trip.

While I was off guiding, Mike or one of the handlers took care of the dogs' basic needs. Still, every night when I got home, no matter how late, I at least walked through the dog yard to visit with my huskies. Sometimes I had time to feed the dogs, too, but I always took that walk to look at my dogs. I just wanted to make sure everything was all right.

In autumn, I use cart training to get the dogs in shape.

CHAPTER 13

FALL TRAINING

Summer is a short season in Alaska. Many summer days here are just as cold and damp as autumn or even winter days in other parts of the country. In Southcentral Alaska, we rarely have any humidity, and a warm summer day means a temperature of about 65 degrees. It is extraordinary if the temperature reaches as high as 80 degrees even once.

My summer felt long only because I was busy every second. The summer is generally down time for the racing dogs. They've got a pretty easy life in the summer. We don't ask much of them. But by August and September, when it is still hot in much of the nation, it is already cooling off drastically in Willow. Then it's time to start building up the racing dogs' workouts again.

In early September, I was training my two racing teams — one full team for the Alpirod and a separate team for the Iditarod. We kept the dogs in cart training — they pull a small, off-road, all-terrain vehicle, a four-wheeler, instead of a dogsled. I sat in the driver's seat as they pulled me through the woods on the dirt trails.

That may sound like fun — and it is — but it's also work. Each year I will travel perhaps 2,000 miles riding a four-wheeler as part

A four-wheeler is my best substitute for a sled when there's no snow.

of dry-land training. I tried to build up the miles on the dogs by using the cart. I was driving five teams a day at one point. Each team would run 10 miles. I was doing 50 miles myself, and running back and forth to the kennel to switch dogs.

Training with a four-wheeler instead of a sled is always a disappointment to me. It's a necessary tool, but it's not really satisfactory. The whole action of the vehicle is not the same as a sled. The dogs don't stretch and feel the same kind of pull and friction with the cart as they do with the sled. I want to be on the sled. Dog mushing is about the whispering sled runners cruising over the hard-packed snow, not wheels crunching and bumping over rocks and roots.

Even in Alaska, you can't depend on the arrival of snow when you need it. The summer of 1993 had been unusually warm and sunny, and some of that warmer weather spilled over into the fall. Around Willow we expect to have one really good snowfall by October 15 or October 20. Not only didn't we get any early snow, but the overnight temperatures didn't dip below freezing with any consistency all the way into November. Even the swampy areas on the network of trails behind my house weren't freezing.

Because the swamps weren't frozen, I couldn't go very far from home without running some risks. I was

"DOG MUSHING IS ABOUT THE WHISPERING SLED RUNNERS CRUISING OVER HARD-PACKED SNOW, NOT ABOUT WHEELS CRUNCHING AND BUMPING OVER ROCKS AND ROOTS."

trapped in Willow, running back and forth on subdivision roads instead of getting out to the backcountry. That gets stale.

I was hemmed into a four-mile route, a loop that sounds like a big circle. But when the dogs were running at a good clip, they completed that loop quickly, so to me it seemed like a small circle. When the dogs were doing 20-mile runs, it got boring. It's like a runner being on an indoor track, doing lap after lap for 20 miles, instead of having the freedom of running the roads or in the woods.

It was a challenge to keep the dogs motivated. You have to keep their mental attitude upbeat. So when their minds started to wander and they grew bored by the same scenery, I had to be careful. I

LEW FREEDMAN

The dog truck is about the most important piece of gear I have.

wanted to keep them happy, but I couldn't let them push me around, either. But you can't discipline them. It's a tenuous time in the training process, and you don't want to discourage them. Besides, what could I really expect? I was asking them to run around in circles.

I had to keep my own outlook positive, too, so I convinced myself that all the dirt running was useful training for the Iditarod dogs because we often face bare ground and uneven terrain in the Farewell Burn during the race. I would play games with myself as we mushed along. I'd say, "Okay, now we're leaving Rohn River on glare ice." Or, "Now we're trying to maneuver in the tussocks." I visualized parts of the trail where the same conditions might prevail, and I used that psychology to boost my own outlook.

It was surprisingly warm well into October and even early November. We had temperatures in the 40s when it normally would have been 25 or 30, below freezing. Then, instead of dropping to colder temperatures and staying there, we had off-and-on weather. It got cold and everything froze. Then it would melt and refreeze. We had a glare ice stage where you could hardly walk around the dog lot without falling on your butt. Even the dogs were falling down when they stepped out of their houses. They couldn't run. They would just slip and fall. The whole neighborhood was a skating rink. It was maddening.

Trying to train on glare ice was amazing. Running alongside the sled, you had to watch every spot where you put your feet down. It's tiring because you have to concentrate so hard. You certainly can't just be running and have your mind off somewhere else. You're thinking about slipping and falling, and it's disruptive. It's hard not to get discouraged.

Typically, in a year when the snow is late arriving, I would pile my dogs in the truck and hit the highway in search of better conditions. I would have driven north, to Fairbanks, or even farther north, to Manley. I definitely would have driven over to Hatcher Pass. Only about 20 miles away, Hatcher Pass is over 3,000 feet in elevation, so it gets snow much earlier than we do in the flatlands.

Hatcher Pass is great. I have run shuttle training trips with different teams up there. I would drive there, unload a team, and mush through the hills. While I was doing that, Mike or a handler would drive the truck back home and load up another group of dogs. I've trained three teams in a day at Hatcher Pass and still slept in my own bed that night.

But I had a complicating problem in the early fall. I had sold my old dog box during the summer, and I was waiting for delivery of a new truck and box. A dog truck is about the most important piece of gear a musher has. The dogs get their own little compartments in the big dog box and recline on beds of straw as you ride along. It's the most efficient and comfortable way for them to travel, like people riding on a train and sleeping in berths.

The new truck was scheduled to arrived in September, but it was a month late. When I really could have used it in October, it still wasn't available. I was stuck at home.

In early November, we finally had a day when it got down to 25 below zero. Then we got our first serious snow in Willow at the end of the month. I was so thrilled. We got six inches, and all I could think was that we were on our way and things would only get better for the rest of the winter. In a lot of areas there were still sticks and bushes poking through the snow. I wasn't comfortable running more than eight dogs on a team at a time, but the snow definitely made it better than running on dirt. Six inches wasn't perfect, but I just about shouted with joy. I loved it. If you want to be a dog musher, you need winter.

Susan Butcher (left) is a tough competitor and a good friend.

CHAPTER 14

SIZING UP THE COMPETITION

Mushing is a solitary sport. You train alone, you prepare alone, you mush alone. Mushers team up with dogs, but they go one-on-one against other mushers.

Often, your only race of the year is the Iditarod itself. That creates an interesting atmosphere. There are always a lot of rumors going around. A lot of gossip. Everybody wonders what everybody else has, how everyone else is training.

In any given year, there are probably sixty to seventy-five mushers who pay the $1,000-plus entry fee to enter the Iditarod. But there are not close to that many mushers who can actually win the race. It's generally accepted that there are about thirty mushers capable of finishing in the top twenty positions that are awarded prize money. And it's generally thought that only ten mushers have a chance to win.

As I began serious training for the 1994 Iditarod, I believed in the general rule of thumb that perhaps ten mushers had the background and fast enough teams to win. I definitely put myself in that category, especially after my second-place finish in 1993.

If you are close to the sport, you can narrow down the field.

Recent history should tell you who will contend in a given year. It's hard to come out of the blue and be a contender in the Iditarod. There are too many good mushers, with too many good dogs, who have invested years in reaching the top.

Obviously, defending champion Jeff King was going to be a contender in 1994. And so was Rick Mackey, who had been right behind us in 1993. You always know that Rick Swenson is going to be in the mix. Rick has the most victories — five — and he had never been out of the top ten in his eighteen races. That's an unbelievable record. An off year for Rick is a great year for most people.

Of course, Susan Butcher, a four-time champion, is going to be a threat every year and everybody knows that. She has a track record that doesn't quite match Rick's, but is the next best thing. People know that if Susan is in the race, she is serious. If there was any question about Susan, it was whether or not she would race. For a few years she had been talking of having a child and taking a break from racing, but every March she made it to the starting line and did well. The 1993 race was the first time I had ever beaten Susan in the Iditarod. When I looked ahead, I assumed she would be in the 1994 race.

In 1992, Martin Buser had been champion, setting the course record that Jeff, Rick, and I broke the next year. I knew Martin would come back strong.

That's six mushers I predicted would be in the top group. Plus, Timmy Osmar from Clam Gulch had been hovering near the front of the pack. He was fourth in 1993, and one of these years he was definitely going to win the Iditarod.

My friend Bill Cotter of Nenana, who had some bad luck in the 1993 race and only finished nineteenth, was someone to watch out for. Matt Desalernos of Nome placed seventh for his highest finish in 1993, but I wondered how much Matt's hard work as Iditarod president had interfered with his ability to train and prepare for the next race. You always have to figure Matt's dogs are going to be strong near the end of the race because they're going home to Nome.

There has never been an Iditarod champion who did not reside in the state. Terry Adkins, who lived in Alaska when the race began but

"MUSHERS CALL EACH

OTHER AND SAY 'HOW'S

YOUR TRAINING

GOING?' PROBING FOR

LITTLE HINTS."

moved to Grand Coulee, Montana, after the first couple of races, has been the most consistent racer from Outside. But in recent years, Doug Swingley of Simms, Montana, has mounted the best challenge amongst non-Alaska residents. Swingley was the rookie of the year in ninth place in 1992, and he moved up to eighth in 1993. He gets a lot of respect, and mushers feel that if anyone is going to become the first winner from the Lower 48, he's the guy to do it.

As the fall continued to be low on snow, weather became a big topic of discussion between mushers. If you think the average person talks a lot about the weather, you can imagine how much a dog musher talks about snow conditions.

The funniest thing that happens as a result of peculiar weather in one part of the state or another is the way the phone lines burn up. All the mushers are trying to psyche each other out. In the fall of 1993, there was a north-south snowfall dividing line. The area north of Denali National Park, which is a good 165 miles from Willow, had plenty of snow, while those of us who lived in Southcentral, in the Matanuska-Susitna Valley or in the Anchorage

Bowl, had bare ground.

So we would hear, "Oh, we've got good training conditions and you've got bad conditions." I'm sure the people in the north, in Fairbanks, were thrilled we were having a hard time training.

Mushers call each other and say, "How's your training going?" Probing for little hints. Joe Garnie's big with that. Every ten days he called. Joe lives in Willow, too, about 10 or 15 miles from me, but he trucked his sleds and dogs out of town, chasing the perfect snow. He would call me and say, "We've been doing 30s and 40s," (referring to his mileage) when he knew I was still on dry land. There I am doing 15s, going in little circles. It's a psyche deal, just part of the game.

It's typical. Everyone's looking for every tiny advantage. Maybe they think if you are five minutes apart, driving for Nome in March, they will have planted a seed of doubt in your mind.

Bob Chlupach is one musher who is such a good friend I can let my guard down when I'm feeling discouraged. I feel I can talk freely with him. We live about across the street from each other.

One day he said, "You know, it's funny. Matt Desalernos' handler calls me about every ten days, and he's always asking how my neighbor is doing."

I said, "You're kidding me."

Bob said, "What neighbor?" Then he laughed and said, "It's always you they want to know about."

So there was this little intelligence-gathering effort going on. The phone company was probably very happy with the long-distance bills.

I thought it was interesting that Matt was trying to find out if I was on schedule with training. I guess that comes with the territory when you finish second. It's a sign of respect, that you really are a threat.

It's crazy the way early snow in one region makes everyone

behave. The year before, in the fall of 1992, Fairbanks mushers were so smug because they had tons of early snow. Everyone had great training up north in October. But the storms didn't stop. The snow kept coming and wiping out their trail system. The volume of snow was so high that it turned into more of a liability than an advantage. Mushers armed with shovels were working harder than their dog teams were.

To be honest, the telephone psyche game worked on me a little. There were days I was frustrated with my situation, and it was getting to me to hear how great someone else had it for training. I was frazzled and I didn't need to hear that.

However, coming off a year when I finished second, and after all of my top-ten finishes, I was a more confident musher. Experience counted here. I referred to all my old training records, comparing where I stood at a given date. I could look back and see how many miles I had on the dogs at a certain point in training, and how fast I went in the Iditarod that year. The records told me that things were really okay, no matter what anyone else said.

Believe me, if you have to depend on your competition to encourage you, you're in trouble. That flat ain't going to happen. We're all friends, but nobody's trying to help the competition be better than they are.

One of the biggest hassles in the Alpirod is trucking from town to town.

CHAPTER 15

LOOKING TOWARD FRANCE

B y the end of November, when we were just starting to get enough snow to completely cover the ground, I was only six weeks shy of leaving for France for the Alpirod.

The Alpirod is one of the biggest events of my year. Although the Iditarod is the biggest race in Alaska and is the best known mushing event worldwide, the Alpirod is the most popular race in Europe. Also, since Royal Canin is one of my main sponsors and the race is important to that company, it's important to my race schedule.

Run through the countryside of France, Switzerland, Italy, Austria, and other European countries, the Alpirod has about as much in common with the Tour de France bicycle race as it does with the Iditarod. Each day is a self-contained, individual stage. The Alpirod is a series of short races laid end-to-end. Although it sounds contradictory, it's really a very long sprint race.

In the Alpirod, we race a specific stage of 40, 50, or 60 kilometers, then awards are presented to the top three for that day's race. At the same time, the times are totalled and we have an overall leader and overall standings. You can win some nice prizes for placing in the top three in the stages, but, of course, the main goal is to win the overall title.

As we go along, we either sleep in designated hotels in that town, or we pack up and move to the next community that hosts a stage. It's a little bit like the circus; we're an event on wheels.

And the Alpirod is a long race. I planned to leave January 10 for the January 15 start in France. The finish was scheduled for January 29 in Italy. Including the prologue, we were looking at seventeen stages of racing, adding up to 920 kilometers — that's close to 600 miles. Obviously, if my dogs were going to be ready, they had to get some good training in with the sled, on good snow.

As Thanksgiving passed and we moved into December, I broke my Iditarod and Alpirod team contenders into five groups and ran five teams a day in training. I still had sixty-two potential racers. In the end, the Iditarod team would have twenty dogs and the Alpirod team would have sixteen.

Running five teams a day was some operation. I was dashing in and out of the dog yard constantly. I was starting to stumble over myself. It was great when Mike could help me out. Otherwise I was running dogs into the night.

Also, as the winter progressed and it got colder, my hand was bothering me again. The metal pin had been removed earlier in the year, but when the wound became really cold, the hand would get stiff and ache. Even more frightening, when it got to be minus 25 degrees and I was out mushing four teams a day, I didn't feel it at all. That's worse. You don't even know you're in danger of getting frostbite. Once I looked down at the hand and it was purple.

My knee still made clicking noises at times, but it was feeling pretty strong and had mostly recovered. Maybe that was a good side effect of not being able to get on a sled until late in the season. I could sit on the seat of the four-wheeler instead of doing all that running alongside the sled on uphills.

Somehow, even with all my training going on, I still had more time than I did most of the year. I could have squeezed in eight hours of sleep a day if I had wanted to, but I had so much on my mind that I couldn't sleep. I was planning all the time, juggling schedules.

It was critical that I put some guts into the Alpirod team. In Europe, the terrain the race organizers use to route the race is very severe, and the dogs are shifting from short stages to long stages. The variance means these sprinters must have some long-distance stamina. The longest single stage in the Alpirod in 1994 was going to be 130 kilometers, about 80 miles. I might have had the fastest dog team in the world, but no one would know if the dogs didn't have the stamina to carry them through the long stages.

To give the dogs an endurance background, I gave them some long training runs early, then I scaled back and used sprint work to sharpen their speed. The end of November and beginning of December was the key time for building up the miles. The fine-tuning process, for the crisp speed, would come during the final weeks of preparation before we flew across the Atlantic.

On top of being a very demanding race physically, the Alpirod is mentally very hard on the dogs, because they are racing hard every day for more than two weeks; some days they even run two stages. What's deceiving is that people look at stages like the prologue, which is just 30 kilometers long or less than 19 miles, and they think, "Oh, how tough can that be? It's just a little sprint race."

But the whole race lasts fifteen days. There isn't another mushing event that lasts that long. If you're near the front of the pack in the Iditarod, you're finishing in ten days, or maybe eleven. That's about five days less than the Alpirod. It's a mental game for the musher and the dogs. Just being out racing day after day takes something out of you.

In the weeks before we left for Europe, I was training five teams a day.

The Alpirod seems to get a little bit longer and more difficult every year. The dual stages are especially nerve-wracking. There may be as few as three hours between races, with a morning start for the first one and an afternoon start for the second one.

Besides worrying about my dogs' preparation, I was concerned about the 1994 Alpirod because I knew it was going to be the stiffest competition I'd ever seen in Europe. Jacques Philip from France, the defending champion who has raced the Iditarod and spends part of the year in Alaska, was coming back. He was the only two-time winner of the race. Grant Beck from Canada, second place the year before, was racing. Tim White from Minnesota was coming back. He hadn't raced in several years, but the last time he entered he won. And Roxy Wright Champaine from Salcha, Alaska, was racing.

Roxy has won so many sprint championships you can't count them. She or her husband Charlie seem to win the Anchorage Fur Rendezvous World Championship every year. Because I mostly stuck to long-distance races and her specialty was sprints, I had never raced against Roxy in any kind of race. I figured Roxy was going to be awesome.

There were also four German dog teams which trained in Alaska. They came for the snow and were smart enough to base themselves farther north than my area, so they had more snow than I did. That was the first time the Germans took the trouble to come to the United States to prepare, so they figured to be a lot better in the race.

In general, even before I went to France, I was beginning to think the Europeans were catching up to the Alaskans, especially in their own sport. Alaskans have been the kings and queens of the trail, but the gap seemed to be closing in the sport of mushing.

I guessed it was going to be hard to make it into the top five of the Alpirod. There were so many knowledgeable drivers with fast teams, who weren't going to be making mistakes, that I knew if I made a mistake it would cost me. It was going to be an unforgiving race.

The 1994 Alpirod started in Autrans, high in the French Alps.

CHAPTER 16
ALPIROD 1994

The Alpirod turned into one of the most amazing mushing adventures I ever had. Things went very well and things went totally crazy. At times it seemed like the race that would never end.

I left Alaska on January 10 for my third try at the Alpirod. The prologue was scheduled for January 15 in a community named Autrans. They had plenty of snow in the French Alps and the whole region, and that meant that the trails were very nice. In past Alpirods, the trails have been bumpy and rutted, not because they aren't well cared for, but because there was a shortage of snow. So it was a pleasant surprise to have abundant snow cover. That would make the racing better and much safer.

It turned out that Autrans was only a sneak preview, as the snow was very good everywhere we went in France. The funny thing was that there wasn't enough snow in other countries that we came to later. A couple of the stages were cancelled because we didn't have enough snow in Austria, of all places.

For this year's Alpirod, there was a field of fifty-three teams, the largest group of starters ever. Roxy Wright Champaine, Tim White, and I were the top Americans, though many other mushers had trained in the United States, including Jacques Philip, who has a home in Willow not far from me.

I knew I had good dogs, that my team was strong. It was well-trained and, despite whatever setbacks that we'd had because of limited snow, I felt as if our overall training had gone well. I felt the dogs were not the speediest team, but our strength would be holding the pace longer than some other teams. I had to think we were pretty ready.

The race began on a high note. I won the 30-kilometer prologue, which is kind of a warmup race. It didn't count in the overall time standings, but it let people know I was there to compete. It established me right away as a contender with the best sprint mushers.

We were one of the first teams out in the staggered start, too, so it felt like we were winning all the way. At the finish line, Roxy came in just one second slower than me. I had never raced against Roxy before, and I never thought I'd be able to beat her in that kind of race. There's a certain amount of awe that you have for the reputation of some drivers, and Roxy deserves that kind of respect for all she has done.

The reception when I won was exciting, too, though I wasn't sure how realistic it was. Everybody was running around congratulating me and saying they hoped I stayed in first. Well, it was a long, long race, and I knew that. I was aware winning the prologue wasn't that big a deal.

And, of course, my day in the sun lasted exactly that long — one day.

The next day, I got crunched. Maybe it was because he was back on his home ground, but Jacques Philip took off and built a huge lead. It got whittled down a little bit before the day was over, but he ran out to a six-minute lead in the standings, just blew us all away. Tim White gained a lot of time on the rest of the field, too, so they established themselves as the front-runners.

Unlike me, Jacques' emphasis is on speed dogs these days, and it really showed. He keeps those dogs really primed. He gobbled up the ground and set the tone for the race. His approach was, "I'm taking the lead, catch me if you can." Ordinarily, you would not want your dogs to go out so fast on the first day for fear they could burn out. But Jacques did it and he was willing to take the risk.

It didn't help any that after my great prologue race I had leader problems on the first stage. My lead dogs just didn't like the traveling that day. I actually had to stop and hook the team down three times to switch leaders. In the Iditarod, coming to a rest and putting the snow hook in isn't that big of a deal because you're in a continuous race. But in this kind of racing, where the stages are shorter, if you stop and put the hook in you know you're not going to win that day. Seconds count, and I lost minutes. So I got behind and spent the rest of the race trying to make up time on Jacques and Tim.

The stages varied. Some days we did 40 kilometers, which is about 25 miles; other days we did 60, 70, or 80 kilometers. There was one very long stage of 130 kilometers. But because of the cancellations, we lost probably 70 planned miles of racing. For me, that was a disadvantage. My team was prepared for a longer race.

There was one new rule in the 1994 Alpirod that I found very interesting. At the start of the race, we named thirteen dogs we were going to be racing. But on any given day we could choose to run anywhere from eight to twelve dogs, resting the others. So we had a pool to work with and could vary the dogs in the team stage by stage.

In the Iditarod, if you start the race with twenty dogs and you drop a dog along the way, you have lost the services of that dog for the duration of the race. But in the Alpirod, where you're driving your team by truck from town to town in between stages, it is just as practical to rest dogs some days, then put them back in the team when they are totally refreshed.

It was all at the musher's discretion how many dogs to run and which dogs to run on which days. I liked that rule. It made for a lot more coaching decisions. For one stage, I made the decision to take only eight dogs because I felt the trail was going to be dangerous and it would be easier to control a smaller team. There were twenty-six road crossings in the stage, and it was supposed to be really icy. As it turned out, the trail was not that bad or that icy, so it hurt me to have chosen a smaller team.

Other aspects of the Alpirod turned out to be nightmares.

Traveling from town to town was horrendous. You had to drive a truck over unfamiliar roads in foreign countries. You were constantly loading and unloading the truck, and maneuvering it in places you didn't know. And in Europe, of course, especially in the old, small towns, they have those tiny, winding streets. They don't have the broad interstate highways we do.

Just imagine how I felt when the front end of the truck fell out in Austria.

It was about a third of the way into the race, not quite a week into it, and the van broke down. Jim Culler, my helper from Alaska, was driving. My mom, Peg Stout, was along as part of the team, and I had another handler. We were driving along at about eleven o'clock at night, wandering all over a small town named Fulpmes in search of the bed-and-breakfast where we were supposed to stay.

We had just turned onto this little road and started uphill when we heard a horrible screeching noise. Jim hit the brakes fast.

The truck literally fell apart. I jumped out and picked up a handful of greasy parts, showing them to Jim. I asked him, "So, what do you suppose all this is?"

Jim got out his headlamp and slid under the truck. "We're not going anywhere," he said.

The driveshaft had disconnected.

Great, huh? It was late at night and there was no one around. We started trying to flag somebody down. We didn't know how to find a tow truck or any other kind of help.

I hated the idea of the dogs being cooped up in the van any longer than necessary. We unloaded the dogs and gear, and hauled them up the hill into this guy's barn. We had all our stuff in the hay. There was no place else to put anything.

"WE HEARD A HORRIBLE SCREECHING NOISE. JIM HIT THE BRAKES FAST. THE TRUCK LITERALLY FELL APART."

Luckily, we didn't have a stage in the morning; it had been cancelled for lack of snow. Otherwise, I could easily have missed the next stage and been forced out of the race.

The other thing we had going for us was that our truck was blocking the road, so we hoped someone would notice us. Still, we sat there for hours in the dark. The night dragged on into the early morning. We couldn't get the truck fixed and we couldn't move it and we couldn't get help. Finally, someone came along and towed it. I don't even know who it was.

This was the all-time insane night. When we got to the bed-and-breakfast, they had given away all our rooms. So we got one room for four people. I slept on the floor — or I lay down on the floor, anyway. I never did really fall asleep.

I was so glad when daylight came, but things were only going to get worse.

We got a ride to Innsbruck and began to search for a new truck. The only vehicle we could rent had to be returned to Austria at the

While racing the Alpirod, my team mushed through many tiny European towns.

end of the race, which wasn't terribly convenient because the Alpirod ended in Italy. Most people wouldn't rent us a vehicle to take to Italy at all because the auto theft rate was so high there.

We had to sign our lives away to get a company to rent us anything. We drove back to Fulpmes to get the dogs and to get on the road to Italy for the next stage.

However, this was not a truck designed for hauling dogs, so we set up the kind of kennel boxes that the dogs use on planes. I had Perry, a three-year-old Alpirod veteran, on a leash and was leading him to the truck when I slipped on the ice. I fell backwards and slammed my elbow against the ground. The leash came out of my hand, and Perry got scared and started to run. The leash was attached to a big, plastic rotary handle at the end. It was popping and banging and making a lot of noise, and that scared him. He really bolted.

I was stunned and had to react fast. I jumped up and we gave chase. Perry just zipped away, out of town, onto the road, into a village, through the center of town, and on to another town. This went on for 20 miles!

It was like a bad dream. I just couldn't believe what was happening. Every once in a while, we would stop and ask if anyone had seen the dog. I was frantic and no one could understand what I was trying to say. Everyone spoke German. Once in a while people would nod their heads and point. They had caught sight of him. We were operating on rumors.

We tracked Perry to this valley where he had passed through, and then, all of a sudden, he was gone. We had no idea where to look next.

I was very upset. Perry is not only a top racing dog who was important to my team, but he is a great dog, one of my babies, and I got very emotional. I didn't want to lose him and I didn't want him to get hurt. On his own, running through the countryside, who knew what was going to happen to him?

We split up in the valley and walked up and down, looking everywhere. I figured Perry was so scared he might be looking for a place to hide. We looked in every barn and under every hay pile. We fought through brush and rugged terrain. On no sleep, we searched for more than six hours.

Most of the day passed, and I had to make a decision. I had to abandon Perry here, get back to the other dogs, and move on to the next stage or I was out of the race. I went to the police and told as many people as I could that I had lost one of my racing dogs and there was a big reward: $2,000. I didn't know what else to do.

I probably hadn't cried that hard for a long, long time. I might have coped better if I knew Perry had been hit by a car, because there would have been nothing I could have done and it would have been over. But the thought of just leaving him, alone and confused, in the middle of nowhere, in a strange place — I just couldn't handle it. I believed in Perry. I knew he was a good, tough dog. I didn't want to give up hope that I would get him back, but there wasn't much evidence to support any kind of optimism.

We sadly loaded up the truck and drove out of Fulpmes. When Perry ran off, it had delayed our departure for the Italian border. Race officials had arranged it so all the mushers and support vehicles would cross in a caravan to minimize any difficulties, but we had missed out on traveling with the group. Knowing that everyone else was gone, I didn't relish the idea of what might happen when we got to the border. I figured they wouldn't even let us through.

When we pulled up to customs, the guy asked, "Are you the girl that lost the dog?"

I said yes, I was, and he said, "The police in Fulpmes have your dog."

They told us to go back to town to get Perry, so we turned around and drove 40 miles, retracing our route.

It was incredible. It turned out that the last farmer we had talked to later thought about a hole in the woods where his brother had fallen in and died. He decided to check the hole for the dog. Well, Perry wasn't in the hole, but when the farmer got to the area, there was Perry, tangled up in some brush, lying perfectly still. Perry is a gray dog and his fur blended in with the brush, so the only thing the farmer could see at first was his blue eyes. But he took him home and contacted the police, and I got Perry back. I did have to pay the $2,000 reward, though. The farmer wanted money for his trouble.

Amazingly, our longest day wasn't over yet. The border guards did let us into Italy, and we rolled along to the next town, Steubaital, which wasn't all that easy to find. Between the search and doubling back, we were hours and hours behind everybody else. We missed the official dinner completely, so we also missed hearing where we were supposed to stay.

I walked the streets of Steubaital in the dark looking for parked official Alpirod vehicles. It took some time to find the right people, then I found out that we had to double back another 12 miles because that's where we were supposed to stay! I was just furious. My nerves were shot.

We drove to the place where we had reservations, and there was no place to park the truck. This neighborhood had teeny, tiny streets. We told Jim to be careful because the road was so narrow, and we didn't like our wide, high truck passing underneath the buildings' overhanging balconies.

"Be careful, be careful," was all we could say and, *boom,* Jim hit a patio. He just bumped it with the top of the truck and kept going. But the guy who lived there came out and started yelling. Then he jumped in his car and chased us. He pulled in front of us, blocking the street, and started screaming for the police.

I knew he wanted money more than justice, but I didn't have any more money. I had spent all the cash rescuing Perry. We did hit his balcony. The truck's blue paint had scraped off on it a little bit, but that was it. He deserved some compensation, but I didn't have anything to give him. It was a Saturday night, and the bank wasn't going to open until Monday. In little places like that, it's not as if there's an automatic bank teller on every corner.

We finally worked it out by having the guy follow us to our hotel, where we convinced the desk clerk to front us some cash. Then we convinced the owner of the house to take the money and not call the police, so at last he went away. By the time I got to the starting line the next day, I was so discombobulated that racing didn't even seem to matter. Everything that had happened would have been stressful enough even if I wasn't in the middle of a race.

That night and day in Austria was the worst of it, but there were other logistical hassles during the Alpirod, too.

It seemed as if we were always running short on gas, but always coming into towns where no fuel was available because it was siesta hour or because we were traveling in the middle of the night.

We were constantly worried we would run out of gas and get stuck by the side of the road in the middle of nowhere where we didn't speak the language.

But there were many good things about the Alpirod as well. The fans were great in many places. They were enthusiastic and loud and, even in some small places, there were thousands of them. We had the biggest crowds in Italy, especially in Cortina, the site of the 1956 Winter Olympics. The fans were ringing cowbells and shouting, just like you saw happening in Norway during the cross-country skiing events at the 1994 Winter Olympics. It was Olympic-style support.

Every day the race competition was fierce, though. Not unfriendly, just tough. After falling behind Jacques and Tim early, my dogs raced better and better. I still think if the race went the full, scheduled distance, without the snow cancellations, I might have been able to pull it out.

Midway into the race, I moved into third, and by the thirteenth stage I had secured third place comfortably. No one was going to come from behind and pass me. I was still trailing Jacques and Tim, but in the longest stage, the 130-kilometer race in Austria, I was within a minute of Tim.

I sprinkled in the occasional stage win along the way, but I never beat those guys by enough time to truly dent the lead. Overall, I placed third. Roxy placed fifth. We finished the race on a cloudy, dark day in Cortina. We mushed through town and up a big hill, so we didn't really finish in front of the fans. They had the awards ceremony later, outdoors right in the middle of the town square. It was very cold and windy, but it was fun because the crowd was noisy and enthusiastic. They were yelling "Bravo! Bravo!"

The Alpirod is a completely exhausting experience to take on when you're trying to prepare for the Iditarod. And for me, it's not even necessarily a profit-making venture. I have to fly myself and the dogs overseas. We pay entry fees, support ourselves, and hope the prize money covers it. This year, between placing third and my stage money payoffs, I won about $15,000 in prize money. That was just about break-even for the event.

Still, I look at the Alpirod as a career-expanding experience. Not only does it give me exposure around the world and the opportunity to meet other mushers, but it makes me sharpen my skills.

By the time I got back to Willow after the Alpirod, it was early February. The start of the Iditarod was barely a month away. It was time to turn my full attention to Alaska's big race.

Before the 1994 Iditarod, we packed food sacks at my parents' house.

CHAPTER 17
FINAL PREPARATIONS

When I got back to Willow after the Alpirod, there were already signs that the 1994 Iditarod was going to be a different kind of race from past Iditarods. The peculiar weather which had plagued early-season training continued: it was too warm.

All over the state, even in the normally coldest regions of the Interior, snow was melting. In February. Some days in Fairbanks the temperature climbed into the 40s! That was unbelievable. The odds were better that it would have been 40 below.

The implications for the Iditarod were serious. The ideal running weather for the dogs is between 20 degrees below zero and 20 degrees above zero. Temperatures in the 40s would be very hard on the dogs. They hate to run in that kind of weather. It's like a human running a marathon with temperatures in the 80s.

But that was only one aspect of how the race would be affected if warm temperatures persisted. The Iditarod Trail crosses many rivers and streams. There are no bridges over those bodies of water. We are able to cross the water only because it's frozen. The dogs, musher, and sled weigh over 1,000 pounds, and deceptively thin ice can be dangerous. A few months earlier, Bruce Johnson, a musher who had competed in the Iditarod and the Yukon Quest, was taking his team on a training run when he fell through the ice and died. A warm weather Iditarod has the potential for disaster.

Not quite as dangerous, but quite uncomfortable for racing, the weather could switch between hot and cold. We could have thawing during the day and freezing overnight. That would make for a terrible trail. Some spots would be icy and slippery, some might be bare, and some would be bumpy. It would mean miserable conditions.

By mid-February, the Iditarod board was alarmed. There was no snow in Anchorage for the start of the race. It had not snowed in Anchorage since the first week in January, just after New Year's. That was a weather aberration bordering on the ridiculous.

A few weeks before the scheduled start of the race on March 5, board members discussed the situation. We felt that it was necessary to preserve some kind of start in Anchorage at all costs for the sake of the thousands of spectators who line Fourth Avenue to cheer us on. Being able to talk to mushers at the start, to shake hands, to wish them well, is the only way local residents can be personally involved. After all, by late evening of the first day, we've usually mushed 100 miles away.

But what were we supposed to do without snow?

Eventually, a contingency plan was drawn up. Normally, when the Iditarod begins, we mush out of downtown Anchorage, along the Glenn Highway, out to Eagle River for about 20 miles. Then we load our dogs in the truck and drive another 30 miles to Wasilla, where a few hours later we hold the official restart. This provides maximum exposure for the people of the most densely populated area in the state. First everyone gets to see us in Anchorage. Then the residents of Palmer, Wasilla, and other places in the Matanuska-Susitna Valley can mingle with us out by the Wasilla Airport.

The new plan called for a truly ceremonial start in Anchorage. Snow would be trucked in and spread on the downtown streets. Mushers would drive their teams past the start banner, as usual, but would only mush a couple of miles to Mulcahy Park. And that would be it for the day. Then the next day we would all truck to the start spot in Willow and begin the race for real. The Iditarod board announced that this new "double start" plan would take effect if the weatherman didn't help out.

"IT'S MY GOAL TO ALWAYS DO BETTER. ONLY ONE SPOT IN THE STANDINGS WOULD ALLOW ME TO SAY I HAD DONE BETTER — FIRST PLACE."

As the clock ticked down to Iditarod Day, weather conditions remained the same. No new snow. The decision was made to implement the new start. And then, of course, as soon as we committed to the new idea, it got colder and we got a huge snowstorm on the last day of February. But we had made the commitment to try the two-day start, so we stuck with that idea.

Meanwhile, I was recovering from the fatigue of racing the Alpirod and the jet lag of my return. I was totally focused on the Iditarod in February, studying the dogs, trying to figure out which ones would make the final team.

Whenever I had a moment to stop working and just sit, I thought about the Iditarod and got butterflies in my stomach. Leading up to the 1993 race, I had been so worried about my own health, I had low expectations for how I would finish. But 1994 was different. I was healthy, stronger than I had been in two years, yet I felt a kind of pressure I never had felt before. It would be very easy to do worse and very hard to do better. And it's my goal to always do better. Only one spot in the standings would allow me to say I had done better — first place. I went into the 1994 race hoping to win. It's what I had worked twelve years to accomplish.

A week or so before the race, I analyzed everything. The team felt great. There were some Alpirod veterans mixed in, and that meant the dogs as a group were faster than ever. They were so fast, it was a little bit scary — not because I wasn't prepared to go fast, but because all the freezing and thawing indicated it might be a slow trail. I wasn't sure the trail could accommodate a fast team.

I was definitely in better shape, having gained confidence from my performance in 1993. For me, having that new level of confidence meant I was less likely to key off how other front-running mushers ran their race. In 1993, I had gone into the race thinking, "Nobody counts but me." That was a new feeling. I had to run my race, by myself. I had to shut the competition off and listen to my body. That turned out to be a blessing in disguise.

Maybe there's some truth in the adage that you have to experience everything in the Iditarod once before you're ready to win. Every year you learn. You learn from the people you travel with, so you can't say that ignoring what they do is always the right decision. Being ready to win, though, is probably different for every musher. That's musher-specific. I think you begin, you learn, you evolve, and then you move into the arena where it's possible to win.

When I finished second behind Jeff King in 1993, I also finished the Iditarod with the second fastest time ever. That made me stronger inside. It gave me the confidence of knowing I can make the good decisions on the trail which lead to a good race. I know that whatever happens, I am wise and experienced enough to make those conditions, or obstacles, or surprises, work for me.

As the 1994 Iditarod approached, I truly felt we were ready to win. We were prepared. I was not dealing with injured dogs or an injured musher. I felt I had overcome any problems in training. I was optimistic.

Maybe, just maybe, 1994 would be my turn in the Iditarod.

At the ceremonial start, my team mushed through the streets of Anchorage.

CHAPTER 18

START AND RESTART

A year after I placed second in the Iditarod, I was back on Fourth Avenue, this time thinking about being first.

So many things were the same as in 1993. I spent the night at my parents' house in Anchorage, a few miles from the starting line. I woke up early. We brought all the dogs downtown. Race officials required us to have all twenty of our dogs there, even though we were only hooking up teams of six dogs.

It seemed funny having just six dogs pull a double sled through town. Double sleds are ordinarily used to prevent the hyped-up dogs from running away with the sled and musher; the extra weight slows them. Using a second sled for just six dogs seemed like overkill.

For the 1994 race start, the atmosphere was unquestionably different than the usual friendly, dramatic, partying feel. I don't think as many fans came out, and they weren't as loud and enthusiastic as they normally were. I guess some people didn't take the new-fangled start seriously.

I was much more relaxed than I usually am for the start of the race. Even for me, there was no getting around the feeling that the real start wasn't for another day, and we were just putting on a show for the people in Anchorage. A typical race start is frantic. This was much calmer. It doesn't take much time to hook up six dogs, and we were only going to be running for about 15 minutes at the most.

So I hooked up the dogs, mushed down Fourth Avenue on a sunny, cool morning, and pulled up to the starting line so they could introduce me to the fans on the loudspeaker. And the public address system went on the blink. The system just went haywire, screaming and screeching. No one could hear me be introduced to the crowd. And, apparently, nobody could figure out how to turn down the sound, so the loudspeaker kept making this horrible noise.

Because of the loudspeaker malfunction, I couldn't get the countdown from officials to tell me to lift the snow hook and mush away. Instead, somebody started yelling to me from the sideline and giving me the countdown — ten, nine, eight — accompanied by hand signals. I couldn't wait to go because the high-pitched sound from the loudspeaker was melting my dogs. They hated it.

Finally, we set off. I mushed down the street, around a few corners, and through town, waving to the people. We mushed down Cordova Hill to Mulcahy Stadium, only a mile or so away. Then we pulled into the snow-covered parking lot and parked. The shortest stage in Iditarod history, I'd say. It was over quickly.

Matt Desalernos had the best comment of the day. He mushed into Mulcahy, put his hook in, and asked a reporter "Who won?"

I got the sense that some of the drivers thought it was silly to go through all the trouble just to mush down the street. But I don't think it was a waste of time. It did show a lot of fans and out-of-town visitors what mushing was like. They could still say they saw a piece of the Iditarod Trail Sled Dog Race. The flavor was still there — dog teams and sleds and barking and dog trucks and the whole nine yards. It just didn't count.

I will say it seemed pretty funny for me to pack up, load the truck, and drive home after starting the Iditarod. The snow conditions prevented us from holding the restart in Wasilla, as we usually do. The new start location was the Willow Community Center, which is only about two miles from my house. Not only did I go home with Mike and the dogs, but a lot of other people spent the night, including handlers, friends, and well-wishers. I think I had about sixteen people at my house that night.

The next day, Sunday, March 6, the 1994 Iditarod began for real.

During the preparations for the start, I felt optimistic, but also cautious and guarded about my chances. I really wondered about the five Alpirod dogs, and about the uneven, hilly terrain we would face in the first 200 miles. Word was that the Dalzell Gorge might be as bad as it had ever been, that the Farewell Burn was at its worst in a decade — bare ground, bumpy ground. When you are mushing a fast team, you need snow to maneuver, to make quick stops, to weave around obstacles . . . basically to use to help you slow down when necessary. In places where there were bare spots and poor snow conditions, I figured it would be hard to stop the team.

To me, the goal was to have a clean start and no problems in the beginning, to deal with the Gorge and the Burn, and cope with any problems that arose, and move on to Nikolai. I felt that once I got to Nikolai, a couple of days into the race, I could deal with anything else that got thrown my way.

For me, it was great having the start in Willow. The restart area in Wasilla is at the local airport, where it's usually quite icy. Because of the location, there are a lot of road crossings and obstacles. You need more control over the team when you're in those situations, so you use a second sled to slow things down for the first 11 miles. But in Willow, we hooked up our twenty dogs and just went. See you in Nome.

Leaving Willow, we had good snow right from the start. We went directly to the backwoods trails, which were wide and flat.

Ordinarily, we face some tough hills going out of Knik towards Flathorn Lake. Instead, we knew we were going to have a nice, clean run for the first 70 miles.

Plus, by starting in the morning, we had daylight for a longer stretch. You could see your leaders and other teams. When you're off with a twenty-dog team and you have light, you can maneuver for passing easily. The whole thing was fun because there were spectators not only massed at the start, but all along the trail.

The route left Willow and went on to Susitna and then to Yentna Station, which was an old Iditarod checkpoint that hadn't been used for a while. Officials turned it into a mandatory stop as a gear check.

In a small place like that, it could have been a disaster with teams bunching up and overcrowding. But the workers did a really good job. They created a system of five different chutes and had a set of handlers to help at each chute. The chutes are narrow spaces lined by temporary fencing, just like you would have at the end of a large running event like the Boston Marathon. The runners are steered into chutes so as they back up they are still able to get accurate places and times. Also, the chutes keep the dog teams apart. Having separate chutes makes it easy to secure your team and snack the dogs while you show officials your equipment.

I don't really know why we had a gear check so soon after the start. We'd only gone 50 miles. But we always have to display mandatory gear at all checkpoints, anyway. It's a safety measure. Mushers also have to pull into designated checkpoints so race officials can chart our progress. And it's a relief from the trail, where dog teams can bed down and rest, and the musher can get a hot meal and some sleep.

I pride myself on my ability to breeze through checkpoints. That's one thing I'm good at. It's a joke on the trail that I'm just a checkpoint kind of girl. The guys joke about that. Jeff King has said he's never seen anyone who's so efficient at a checkpoint as I am. In a close race, time spent in checkpoints can separate the winner from second place. I learned that from Susan Butcher. I watched Susan operate in checkpoints for years. She was always remarkably efficient and made every minute count. Thoughout the 1994 race, I worked to maintain my speed through the checkpoints.

"I WAS DRIVING A TEAM THAT WAS FASTER AND MORE POWERFUL THAN ANY I'VE EVER HAD. TALK ABOUT YOUR MIXED BLESSINGS."

Even though it was well organized at Yentna, it was quite a mob scene. You had barking dogs and handlers and mushers. I did my thing and mushed back out onto the trail and, though I could hardly tell in all the confusion, I had taken the lead. Nobody else was out of Yentna yet.

I didn't realize I was ahead until Jeff King passed me. He said, "We'll have to stop meeting like this."

There we were, right where we left off in 1993, running one-two in the Iditarod. Jeff took the lead and some miles later, Martin Buser, the 1992 winner, passed me heading into Skwentna. Since the Iditarod is such a long endurance race, it's common for a group of front-runners to constantly exchange the lead.

So things did go as smoothly as possible at first. But thoughts of the Burn flitted through my mind. Rookies who travel through the Burn can't imagine the hassles and the difficulty of handling a sled being tossed side-to-side on steep ground. There's such a thing as too much knowledge, I guess. I've had a sled demolished in the

Burn. I've fallen in the ice. I've been dragged across glare ice trying to figure out how I'm going to get my leaders to see something that isn't really there — a trail.

And I was driving a team that was faster and more powerful than any I'd ever had. Talk about your mixed blessings. It's great to have power and speed. That's what you need to win. But that's one tricky thing about the Iditarod: the rugged conditions do not always favor the fastest.

I guess I'm a worrier. Plan for the worst, hope for the best.

It was Sunday afternoon, before dark, when we got to Skwentna. The pace was fast, but comfortable. Whenever we had flat ground and good snow, we were flying — not just me and my dogs, but all the mushers at the front. We didn't let anything slow us down, right from the start. It was no surprise to me. In recent years, we seem to break records at just about every Iditarod. In 1994, we were moving at record speed right out of the chutes.

Good snow on the first day of the race soon gave way to warmer weather.

CHAPTER 19

THE LONG STRETCH

You do not associate hot weather with the Iditarod Trail Sled Dog Race. The image is one of overpowering cold and storms. But in the first two days after I mushed out of Skwentna, traveling between Finger Lake and Nikolai, it warmed up to the 40s! The clouds hung densely, and it was humid.

I couldn't believe it. During my last stretch of training, the temperature reached 30 degrees below zero. Now I was caught off guard by the heat.

I learned that some of my dogs were too heavy. Many of the dogs bred for the Iditarod team — not the Alpirod transplants — were about five pounds too heavy for slogging through the soft snow. I thought that 50 pounds would be the perfect weight for the dogs, but I was wrong. Five extra pounds out of fifty is a lot — 10 percent. It's too much.

Several of the dogs with this problem were my key dogs, proven Iditarod leaders like Barkley, Sissy, Patches, and Maverick. The race pace was very fast, and the Alpirod dogs were cruising along quite comfortably, hitting the right speed easily. But some of the Iditarod dogs had to extend themselves in the warm weather, on the mushy trail. If they had weighed a little bit less, they might not have had the same difficulty. They were straining to match the pace.

It was too much work, too soon, under trying conditions. Instead of us working smoothly as a unit and keeping in touch with the other top teams, we were struggling. The workload was too much and some of the dogs overheated.

I began the race with a team of what I considered to be trail-tough dogs, and all of a sudden several of my best dogs had to go in the sled for a rest. In my twelve years in the Iditarod, I had packed only one or two dogs into checkpoints. In the first quarter of the 1994 Iditarod, I carried eight dogs in the sled at one time or another. They all needed breathers. I didn't have a clean run for seven days. I was either packing a dog or in the process of dropping a dog all the way to McGrath, about 400 miles into the race.

And that wasn't the end of it, either. I had to drop another dog at Cripple, which is about 120 miles beyond McGrath. It was continual. It was a pattern with the team for the whole race.

It was flabbergasting to watch everything we had trained for fall apart. Every year you plan and evaluate, trying to figure out how you can improve, trying to predict what might occur. But sometimes things happen that are just the luck of the draw; you have no control over them. Something completely new is thrown at you, and it changes everything.

However, you can't panic. You can't give up. You have to have enough versatility in your dog team so you can respond with the strengths of other dogs. I had dropped some of my best dogs, so it was up to other dogs in the team to carry the load. It's the same situation as a basketball team might face. The star player gets injured, so the team has to rely on guys coming in off the bench. I felt like I had backups who could do the job.

Still, I was definitely frustrated. I was particularly bothered when I loaded Perry into the sled going into Rainy Pass. He was always loping instead of holding his stride, so I knew he was going to have to ride, not run. I couldn't figure out what was wrong. When the veterinarian checked him, he said sore feet was the only thing he could find.

The only explanation that I could think of was that Perry was an Alpirod dog. He's young, and maybe being out on the trail wore him down a little bit. When his feet got a trifle sore, he reacted strongly. Whereas one of the trail-tough Iditarod dogs might not even notice sore feet, Perry wasn't used to this kind of endurance run. He probably thought he was dying.

"SOMETIMES THINGS HAPPEN THAT ARE JUST THE LUCK OF THE DRAW. . . . SOMETHING COMPLETELY NEW IS THROWN AT YOU, AND IT CHANGES EVERYTHING."

The high temperatures hurt Iditarod dogs like Maverick and Barkley. Maverick was dropped. I had Barkley checked by vets twice in Rainy Pass, once when we first arrived and once just before we left. The vets did not recommend dropping him. I was told he was overheating, but that it wasn't a big problem.

As we approached the Dalzell Gorge, I took a rest with a group of other mushers. Rick Swenson, Rick Mackey, Jeff King, Martin Buser, and I sat around talking about what a nightmare it would be to carry a dog in the sled down into the Gorge. Martin said something like, "Well, what about two dogs?" We all laughed and said sure, that would never happen.

And immediately after that, I had to pack two dogs in the sled

©1994 JEFF SCHULTZ

Two of my hard-working huskies took a quick nap along the trail.

through the Gorge.

The forecast passed on to me said that the weather would cool down overnight. Well, it didn't cool down. It stayed just as warm or got even warmer. So when the team started down into the Dalzell Gorge, we sped up with the downhill momentum. Barkley overheated again, he went down, and he had to go into the sled. Sissy also had to go into the sled. She wasn't running well.

There I was, right in the rock crevasse of the Gorge, stopping to load dogs. That's not great. Carrying dogs in the sled down the Gorge was even tougher. This was steep, narrow trail, never going straight. Sometimes I had to quickly throw the sled up on one runner to get around trees and to keep from crashing into them. I had almost 100 pounds of dogs in the sled, in addition to 100 pounds of gear that I was trying to throw around like a gunny sack.

Just the added poundage makes such a difference. I'm not a big person with tremendous upper body strength. I'm not that tall, so I don't have much leverage. And I definitely didn't have power steering. Luckily, neither Barkley nor Sissy tried to fight me. They behaved.

I was happy to get on down the Gorge and get back to concentrating on racing with Martin Buser, Bill Cotter, and Jeff King. When I pulled into Rohn, Bill looked at me and told me he couldn't believe I had done that.

Who would imagine that after so many years in the Iditarod I would have a new experience? Not a good experience, but a new one.

Coming out of Rohn River, there was so far to go. I didn't want to carry any more dogs. I dropped Patches, a three-time Iditarod finisher, because she wasn't eating or drinking. Sissy had led my team for half the race in 1993, and I had to drop her. Maverick was gone. Barkley had led the team into Nome in 1993, and now he was gone, too. I was leaving behind experienced, veteran dogs.

From a distance, fans following my progress could tell that something was wrong with my team just by watching the number of dogs diminish. What neither the fans nor the other mushers could know was how important those dogs were to me. I had come into the race with the best dogs from my kennel, and by dropping them within 200 miles, essentially benching them for the duration of the race, I was losing leaders, dogs with talent and experience.

When I had already dropped four dogs by Rohn River, it changed my expectations. I came into the race dreaming of becoming champion of the Iditarod in 1994. Now my main goal became finishing in the top five. I still felt like that was not out of the realm of reality. After packing the dogs so much early on, I was hoping to have clean runs straight through.

What happened later was that the dogs still running paid for hauling extra weight in the sled. Packing so much weight over such a long period of time ground the speed out of the team.

I was hopeful until we got to Unalakleet. There is less than 300 miles to go at that point, and that's where the race is determined, where the front-runners start separating. Everything started catching up to me on the Bering Sea Coast.

I mushed into the village of Unalakleet with only nine dogs. Riding in the sled was my last true coastal leader, the last dog left on my team that had the experience of mushing the Iditarod Trail's last few hundred miles. I had to leave that dog behind in Unalakleet, and turn to the coast for the final third of the run into Nome with no coastal leader. That was foreboding.

Suddenly, I had Elroy as my main leader, a dog that I had intended to be mainly an Alpirod dog. He was the only leader available, and he came through in a big way. He rose to the occasion, taking charge of the team, showing us the way home to Nome. I would have liked to give him some time off from leading, because it's hard work, but I really relied on Elroy.

I also used Sheena in lead because it was necessary. She excelled, really over-excelled compared to what I had thought her capabilities were. Somewhere she found the strength and the smarts, and she dug it out and gave it all to me. I think Elroy's confidence helped. I've raced Sheena for years, and I didn't see her as a main leader. Some of Elroy's sureness rubbed off on her. They made a good pair.

People have asked me if, when things went bad, I ever considered quitting the race. That was never a consideration. I was not in jeopardy. I was not close to dropping out. I might have gone slower, I might have fallen back in the standings, but I was going to get to Nome.

Even after the early stretch when I dropped so many dogs, we were mushing fast. I couldn't really believe how fast the pace was, especially since the trail was bad. It had melted and refrozen, and was nothing like the training trails we used in the middle of winter near Willow. My dogs never had to take care of themselves on bad trails before the race. I could have forced them to train on poor terrain, but I didn't want to risk unnecessary injuries. I pride myself that I don't cripple dogs in training. Now my dogs had to face bad trails for the first time in the Iditarod, with everything at stake.

Once again, it became a case of adapting to circumstances, of making do. I mushed along on the cold nights, on the sunny days, and kept telling myself, "Top five, top five."

We had been through a lot, but I trusted my dogs to get me to Nome.

CHAPTER 20
THE FINISH LINE

Two-thirds of the way into the race, mushing on the frozen Yukon River over the 90-mile stretch between Kaltag and Unalakleet, there were nine mushers still in contention for the championship. I was having problems, but I was one of those nine. Martin Buser seemed to have the strongest team. And Rick Mackey seemed to be in the best position to challenge him.

That is one misleading thing about the Iditarod for fans. They read the standings and read the times, and they see mushers bunched together. They feel anyone has a shot at winning.

This is only theoretically true. Yes, we were close together in places. But when you are traveling with other mushers, you can sense what is happening in their teams. You can count their dogs. When a team pulls out of a checkpoint an hour behind you and passes you within two hours, you know that team is stronger than yours at that moment.

The Iditarod is a long race and anything can happen, but it is a race of attrition. By the time you reach Unalakleet, you pretty much know what you have going for you and what the other top mushers have going for them.

I was not giving up, but I was getting pretty realistic. My goal of winning the 1994 Iditarod had slipped to hoping to finish in the top five. Now it was slipping even more, to hoping to place in the top ten.

Of the nine teams fighting for first place, my team had suffered the most problems. Just keeping up with the group was a monumental effort for me. My dogs were wearier than the others' dogs because there had been fewer of my dogs doing the work for a long period of time. Mine was definitely the most compromised team in the group.

If I had been able to build a lead over some of the others, like Charlie Boulding, Doug Swingley, or Tim Osmar, I think I could have stayed ahead of them, held them off. But I was unable to make that kind of charge, to make any kind of spurt to put distance between myself and them. It wasn't to be.

I was interested in moving up. I wanted to do better. But as I mushed along, passing through the Native villages of Shaktoolik and Koyuk, my goal became hanging on to ninth place. If someone had trouble in front of me and had to slow down, fine, I'd pass them and I'd take that as a bonus. But the harsh reality was that ninth was the best I could hope for if nothing changed the big picture.

And, of course, especially along the coast, the big picture often does change in a hurry. A dog team might suffer from a spreading illness. Dogs might get tired. The most likely scenario would be the arrival of a huge storm. That could slow down the front of the pack and bunch everybody up. It could enable me to catch up to other teams and gain some rest.

Powerful storms that paralyze the race are frequent occurrences during the final hundred miles of the Iditarod. In 1991, it was a foregone conclusion that Susan Butcher had the best team leaving White Mountain and that her lead was insurmountable. She was sure to win her fifth Iditarod. But it did not happen. A storm came in, disrupting the race, and Rick Swenson ended up winning his fifth Iditarod instead.

So I could see good reasons to root for a vicious storm. Sometimes big storms work to your strategic advantage. The pace of the 1994 Iditarod was blistering, so unless something happened to slow down the race, I wasn't going to be gaining on anybody. I was totally focused on keeping my team together, on not having any other dogs become so tired they couldn't continue.

"OF THE NINE TEAMS FIGHTING FOR FIRST PLACE, MY TEAM HAD SUFFERED THE MOST PROBLEMS. JUST KEEPING UP WITH THE GROUP WAS A MONUMENTAL EFFORT."

At this point, I was just thinking of making it to Nome in a respectable fashion.

As we turned to Nome, coming out of the little villages, I had to pump my foot constantly on the flats to help the dogs move, instead of riding on the runners with both feet. Going uphill, I had to get off the sled and run beside the team. It was the only way for us to make time. I was just like another husky out there. I was nursing the team home. If I didn't urge the dogs forward, especially going uphill, they would just stand there.

It was a good thing nothing like this happened during the 1993 race. Given my knee's condition, there was no way I could have run alongside like that, or been kicking constantly on the back of the sled. This year, luckily, both my knee and my hand had healed and didn't slow me down.

But running as much as I did and pumping so hard did wear me out. And I didn't do a great job of taking care of myself. In ten days I had only twenty hours of sleep — seven hours in Nikolai and only thirteen hours the entire rest of the race. Another problem was not drinking enough water. You can monitor your intake of fluids better when you are coasting along on the back of the sled. But when you're pushing and running, you tend to let it slide. I didn't keep up with my needs.

It had been years since I was so tired that I hallucinated on the trail, but I was hallucinating near the end of the race. I first started hallucinating mushing into White Mountain, which is two checkpoints from Nome. As I was mushing, I had the sensation I was going into a tunnel. The trail seemed narrower. Everything would get real narrow and then it would widen up again and then get real narrow. It was as if the terrain shifted, as if someone was playing a trick on you. I had more hallucinations headed into Safety, and again from Safety to Nome.

The fast pace was a contributing factor in the fatigue, too. There was simply less time to squeeze in some sleep. You're always trying to grab naps on the Iditarod Trail, but it seemed like the race was moving non-stop. Nobody had much time to sleep. With all the problems with my dogs, I spent extra time on the trail fighting to stay even.

Just between Unalakleet and Shaktoolik, most of the teams covered the 40 miles in six and a half hours, and I took seven hours. That was typical of my runs near the end. Their pace was wearing me down.

I had the choice of resting for a long period of time and picking up some speed coming off the rest, or I could virtually make myself part of the team, have us slow down, but also have us keep going. For me, the difference during the last third of the race was probably going to be racing at seven miles an hour or racing at nine miles an hour. I chose to slow down and make as much progress as we could, stopping as little as possible.

"Slow is fast, if you're moving." That's a saying of Terry Adkins', and that was my story. You've got to keep going. If you stand still, someone might come up from behind.

When you are racing in the Iditarod, you are on an incredible journey. It seems like a never-ending journey at times. The trail becomes your whole world, and your immediate world is the dog team. You are totally focused on the dogs and their health and on your own condition and health. It is the only way you can exist. The pace is fast, and you live from one checkpoint to the next. You develop a rhythm, blocking out distractions or anything that doesn't relate specifically to making progress.

In White Mountain, with 77 miles to go or about eleven hours of mushing, I was feeling pretty upbeat because we were coping. I had problems, I faced them, and I solved them. Problem, solution. Problem, solution. New obstacle? I can do this. I'll do this. I'll try this. I'll try that.

I was fighting off any disappointment about not being higher in the standings by devoting all of my attention to getting to the finish line. Often your mood translates to the dogs, so I wanted to make sure they didn't get down. I couldn't afford to have that happen.

One way I accomplished that was by snacking them almost constantly. I snacked my dogs an incredible amount the 55 miles between White Mountain and Safety. I even snacked them three times between Safety and Nome, the last 22 miles. It wasn't for nutrition, but because I thought it would be helpful mentally. The snacks were mental pick-me-ups, messages of "Keep going, boys, we're almost there."

I held onto ninth place.

I crossed the finish line on Front Street in Nome in 11 days, 4 hours, 25 minutes. That placed me just behind Tim Osmar and just in front of Susan Butcher.

Martin Buser won the race and set a new record of 10 days, 13 hours, 2 minutes. Rick Mackey was second, Jeff King third, Rick Swenson fourth, and Bill Cotter fifth. Doug Swingley, in sixth, and Charlie Boulding, in seventh, also beat me.

I finished with nine dogs in harness, having dropped eleven of my twenty dogs along the way. My prize was $12,000.

I have never been so happy to get to Nome. I was frustrated and exhausted and when I stood there at the finish, answering reporters' questions, all my fatigue and worries hit me at once and I burst into tears. I'd never had a year on the trail like that. I was totally worn out. All of my competitors have had races where things didn't go as well as they had planned. The 1994 race was my turn.

One of the newspaper stories said that I looked bedraggled, and that was how I felt. My hair was a mess. I needed a bath. My whole body ached. I was so tired. I felt like being immersed in a bathtub for a week and just soaking and sleeping.

I couldn't really even think clearly until I got some sleep. I went over to the house where Mike and I stay in Nome and I just collapsed. I slept a lot the next couple of days.

When you are fatigued and falling behind during the race, you have to fight off feelings of depression. But on the morning after I finished, when I woke up in Nome, I was even more down. I realized there was nothing more I could do. It was over. There wasn't another problem to face or beat. No more miles to make up distance. No more miles to the finish. I had been pumped up, adrenalin flowing, and now I was done. That's it for this year, Dee. That was the hardest moment for me. I really felt the post-race letdown in 1994. You always do, but this was more severe than ever.

It wasn't until I got some rest and recovered a little bit that I had any time to think through what had happened. I was very proud of completing the race and finishing ninth. True, it was not what I was hoping for back at the start in Anchorage, but given what happened, I did a good job on the trail.

©1994 JEFF SCHULTZ

We pulled into the finish chute on Front Street in 11 days, 4 hours, 25 minutes.

The good thing was that there was no permanent injury to any dog. Some of the dogs overheated and I had to drop them, but they bounced right back. No dog was lame, or stiff, or even still sore a week after the race. Sometimes what seem like little injuries — causing a limp and knocking a dog out of the race — can turn out to be much worse and end a racing career, but none of that occurred.

There were no long-term negative implications for the team. In fact, the way it worked out, with several two-year-olds being pressed into demanding roles and coming through, the future of the team looked brighter. When the pressure was put on the young ones, when I really needed them to come through, they did it for me.

The dogs could have folded, in which case I wouldn't have finished ninth, and they might never have wanted to race again. But they rose to the occasion and really shined. I feel really good about that. My faith in those dogs was definitely rewarded. Also, those young ones had five more brothers and sisters back home who hadn't made the Iditarod team. Those dogs could have great potential.

What seems apparent now is that Elroy has become my next great leader, like Johnnie was before him. Elroy is six years old, and he has fifty-six stages of the Alpirod behind him and two Iditarods. No more Alpirod racing for Elroy. It's too much to ask him to do both. If he could have voted right after the race, he probably would have chosen to go to the Alpirod instead of the Iditarod, but I'm convinced Elroy has become an Iditarod dog.

The entire 1994 Iditarod brought home to me one aspect of endurance racing: in order for you to win, things have to go perfectly. Or close to perfectly. There's a little bit of luck involved. Things have got to go your way. And if they're not going your way, then something major has to happen to slow the whole race down. If we had a storm, perhaps forcing everybody to sit in one place for twenty hours, it could have been a different story for me.

Perhaps my real lesson for the 1994 Iditarod was that you can't give up. I've known that for some time, but I guess I really hammered that notion home this time. If you allow yourself to give in, to stop fighting, the race just seems longer, the miles get longer, the days pass slowly, and every hill is so much higher. You simply can't allow yourself to stop trying. The only time you stop pushing is when you pass under the burled arch in Nome.

The Iditarod brings out the best in you.

EPILOGUE

E very time you race in the Iditarod, you learn something.
You take something with you from every experience in life,
and no matter how many times you race the 1,100-mile
trail, you should learn something from the test, either about yourself
or about getting better at what you do.

In the 1994 race, I learned a lot about pacing myself and the
dogs. The key thing about the dogs was how to assemble a unit.
This was the first time I tried to switch Alpirod dogs over to the
Iditarod team.

I originally started out with a committed Alpirod team and a
committed Iditarod team. Most of the dogs in each unit had been
working together for four months, but the Alpirod dogs who raced
in both races did not have a full Iditarod background. They were
only part of the Iditarod team for four weeks. With twenty-twenty
hindsight, I think that it was a mistake to mix them up. The trail
itself wasn't conducive to using the faster runners. I had to learn
that. If you don't take the chance, you never know what will work
or not work.

When the Iditarod ended, I was deflated, but when I got some
rest, got home, and thought about it, I realized that it should always
be exciting just to be part of an event like that. When I think about

what we accomplish — and I mean all of the drivers — I am uplifted. Nobody, unless they have been out on the trail, can really understand the challenge of the Iditarod, the beauty of the land, the friendship between the competitors. It really is something special.

The Iditarod is such an Alaskan event. It's linked to the mystique of the country, the history of the state. Mushing is the way the frontier was challenged. There is a lot of romance in being part of the Iditarod.

And the Iditarod is about being tough. You think you're tough? Well, try this. This is tough. Part of being in the Iditarod is just successfully negotiating your way to the end of the trail. How many people ever do anything that tough in their lives? When it's snowing, people stay home. When it's cold, people stay in the house by the fire. We're out there in every weather condition, fighting the elements. This is not in the realm of most people's experience.

We do have disappointments because all of us want to be first. But when things go wrong, we finish it out. We still want to get to Nome, no matter what happens to us along the way. A few years ago, Lavon Barve was separated from his team in a storm and walked for hours to find them. He was reunited with the dogs and pressed on, finishing the race. A similar thing happened to Joe Garnie. They showed what it's all about. You go for it and stay in it to the end if you possibly can. I was pleased I stuck with it and got to Nome.

I thought about Bob Ernisse, an Anchorage guy who had a long-time goal of racing and finishing the Iditarod. When he raced a couple of years ago, he was trapped by a storm about 30 miles from the end and couldn't finish. The storm that trapped him in his sled basket outside of Safety could have killed him. He was taken to the hospital with frostbite and hypothermia. Think of that. He was only 30 miles from completing his dream. That's all his dream was, just finishing, and he ran the risk of dying.

And yet in 1994, he came back to the Iditarod to finish out his dream. He had to travel more than 1,000 miles just to cover that last distance on the trail and say he did it all. Who would have blamed him if he never raced again? Everybody understood why he had to withdraw that first time. It was a matter of life and death. Nobody expected him to go back and invest another whole season of training. And he came back and did it again.

Then, in his second race, Bob fell way back and ran into another storm. To have another storm hit him in the face when he was only a few miles from Nome again, just as he was about to finish, was almost unbelievable. And still the guy pushed through.

I was standing on the street when he came into the finish chute and I was just so proud of him. Bob could have hugged everything in sight. He was so happy. He hugged me two or three times that night at the finishers' banquet. He just couldn't digest that he really did it. He felt so good. And he should have. How many times do we let things in life get us down without our fighting back?

I'd like to think that it was admirable that I could finish ninth in 1994. Even though 1993's second-place finish might have looked pretty, finishing ninth in 1994, given the circumstances, was quite an accomplishment, too. It was just done under a whole different set of circumstances.

The Iditarod makes you reach inside yourself. It brings out the best in you. A lot of times, if you don't have something outside of yourself to make you reach, you don't realize what you can accomplish. If, while I was at home, somebody told me that for the next ten days I could only sleep two hours a night, I'd probably say I couldn't do it. But I did it during the 1994 Iditarod.

I guess I can do that if I have to, when I have something I want to accomplish that requires that level of commitment. For me, the dogs are that passion. If taking care of my animals requires me to stay awake, I can do it. If it's just staying awake so I can read a book, I can't. But I have enough drive in myself to provide for my dogs, to

The lessons I learned will help me have stronger teams in the future.

make sure they are okay. I would rather help them than sleep. That's my internal drive.

After I got back to Willow following the 1994 Iditarod, I slept hours and hours every day for about a week. Sleep helped my outlook and attitude a lot. It took a week, but I finally got back to normal. And as soon as I felt better, I started thinking about the 1995 Iditarod and planning for it.

One thing will certainly be different about the 1995 race. At the breakup banquet following the 1994 race, Susan Butcher announced she was retiring from the Iditarod. Susan has four Iditarod championships and, through her success in the race, has become a national figure. Entering the race every year from 1978 to 1994, she had fifteen top-ten finishes.

It was a surprise that she made the announcement so firmly, but

Susan has hinted for a few years that she needs to step back from the Iditarod and take a break. I think Susan, at age thirty-nine, reached a point in her life where she wanted to spend some time with her husband and have a life away from intense dog racing.

Susan was a big help to me over the years. I learned a lot from being around her and racing against her. She set a standard of accomplishment that's going to stand for a while. She has also been a confidant of mine, and I'm going to miss the camaraderie we've had.

The departure of Susan Butcher means there will be one less contender chasing the right to be called champion of the Iditarod. But all of the other top contenders are sure to be back. No doubt there is someone out there who has been accumulating experience, who is ready for a breakthrough.

Within a week after the end of the 1994 Iditarod, I started running young dogs again. I felt renewed and refreshed and excited about the talent I saw in the dogs. I got back into the routine pretty quickly, and it was still fun. Thinking about Susan getting out of the race, I concluded that when it's no longer fun anymore, you shouldn't do it. You shouldn't mush dogs, you shouldn't race races, you really shouldn't do anything if you can't say you're having a good time.

Looking around the dog yard, listening to the dogs bark and pull at their chains, I heard them telling me they wanted to run. And I wanted to go, too. I hooked up a team and we mushed out of the yard, dashing into the trees. I stood on the back of the sled, and I thought, "Wow, this is good, this is fun." I felt as alive and excited as ever.

Within a few more days, I was looking ahead, planning my breeding program and evaluating the dogs I already had. The more I thought about the dogs who made it to the finish line in 1994 and the other up-and-coming dogs, the better I felt about my chances for the 1995 race.

I honestly think my dog team is better than it ever has been before. That doesn't guarantee me a victory in the Iditarod. But it does tell me that when I move onto the starting line, I'll have the kind of dog team that can win. DeeDee Jonrowe will be a better musher, and the dogs will be better racers.

I'll definitely have a fighting chance to win in 1995, and there isn't any more you can ask for than that.

TREATMENT OF IDITAROD DOGS

"I'm sure that the average Iditarod dog gets better care than 99 percent of the dogs in America. . . . Iditarod dogs are fed the best food. . . . They get regular feedings each day and regular exercise. As far as I'm concern, my dogs are members of the family."

—DeeDee Jonrowe

The rules of the Iditarod are designed to insure not only fair competition between mushers, but the humane treatment of all sled dogs. Following are some condensed excerpts from the official 1995 Iditarod rules.

Dog Care: A musher will be penalized if proper dog care is not maintained. Dogs must be maintained in good condition. All water and food must be ingested voluntarily.

There will be no cruel or inhumane treatment of dogs. Cruel or inhumane treatment involves any action or inaction which causes preventable pain or suffering to a dog.

Qualified Dogs: Only northern dog breeds suitable for arctic travel will be permitted to enter the race.

Number of Dogs: A musher may start the race with no more than sixteen dogs (previously twenty dogs) and no less than twelve dogs. At least five dogs must be on the tow line at the finish line. No dogs may be added to a team after the start of the race. All dogs must be either on the tow line or hauled in the sled. No dogs may be led behind the sled or allowed to run loose.

Sled: A musher has a choice of sled or toboggan to be drawn. The sled or toboggan must be capable of hauling any injured or fatigued dogs under cover, plus equipment and food.

Harness and Cables: Dogs must leave checkpoints with functional, non-chafing harnesses. A musher must carry tie-out lines or have cable in their towline capable of securing a team.

Mandatory Items: A musher must have with him/her at all times the following items:

1. A proper cold-weather sleeping bag weighing a minimum of five pounds.

2. An ax with a head to weigh at least one and three-quarter pounds, and a handle at least 22 inches long.

3. One pair of snow shoes with bindings, each shoe at least 264 square inches in size.

4. Any promotional material provided by the Iditarod Trail Committee.

5. Eight booties for each dog.

6. One operational cooker and pot capable of boiling at least three gallons of water.

7. A veterinarian notebook, to be presented to the veterinarian at each checkpoint.

Gear will be checked at all checkpoints except Eagle River, Wasilla, Knik, and Safety.

Dog Food: A minimum of 74 pounds of dog food per dog must be distributed among seventeen checkpoints along the trail.

Veterinary Pre-race Examination: A musher must have the team examined at the official pre-race veterinary examination or must deliver proof of examination by an Iditarod-approved veterinarian. All dogs entered in the race must have current distemper, parvo, corona, and rabies vaccines, and must be wormed for Echinococcus. No dogs may be switched after the pre-race veterinarian check.

Veterinary Care: Dogs are under the jurisdiction and care of the chief veterinarian and the veterinarian staff from the time they enter the staging area until 72 hours after the team finishes in Nome or scratches or is disqualified. A veterinarian may prevent a dog from leaving a checkpoint or the starting line for medical reasons.

Drug Use: No injectable, oral, or topical drug which may suppress the signs of illness or injury may be used on a dog. No drugs or artificial means may be used to drive a dog to perform beyond its natural ability. Mushers may not inject any substance into their dogs.

Dogs are subject to the collection of urine or blood samples, at the discretion of the testing veterinarian, at any point from the pre-race examination until four hours after the race finishes in Nome.

Mandatory Stops: A musher must take one 24-hour stop (previously one 30-hour stop) during the race. The 24-hour stop may be taken at the musher's option at a time most beneficial to the dogs. In addition, a musher must take one eight-hour stop on the Yukon and one eight-hour stop at White Mountain.

Hauling Dogs: A musher may haul dogs in the sled at his/her discretion. However, the musher may not allow any of the dogs to be hauled by another team. Dogs must be hauled in a humane fashion and must be covered if conditions require. Coverage is mandatory when windchill is below +20 degrees Fahrenheit.

Unhealthy Dogs: All injured, fatigued, or sick dogs that are dropped from the race must be left at a designated dog drop. Any dropped dog must be left with four pounds of dog food and a reliable chain or cable with swivel snap and collar.

Expired Dogs: Any dog that expires on the trail must be taken by the musher to a checkpoint. A necropsy will be carried out to determine the cause of death and whether the musher should continue, continue with penalty, or be withdrawn or disqualified.

Penalties: Policy and rule infractions may result in issuance of warnings, monetary penalties, time penalties, censure, or disqualification. Mushers shall be disqualified for rule infractions involving physical abuse of a dog, such as kicking or beating, or for other acts involving cruel and inhumane treatment.

ABOUT THE AUTHORS

Lew Freedman, 43, is a native of Boston. He graduated from Boston University with a degree in journalism, then served as a staff writer on various newspapers, including the *Philadelphia Inquirer*. Moving to Alaska in 1984, he became the sports editor of the *Anchorage Daily News* in May of 1985. Freedman has written prize-winning short fiction, he has received dozens of journalism awards, and his work has been included three times in the *Best Sports Stories* anthology. He lives with his wife Donna, a feature writer at the *Daily News*, and daughter Abby in Anchorage.

DeeDee Jonrowe, 41, has loved dogs for as long as she can remember. Her family moved to Alaska when she was seventeen, and she became interested in sled dog racing while attending the University of Alaska Fairbanks. A competitor in twelve Iditarod races, Jonrowe has finished in the top ten for seven consecutive years, with a best finish of second in 1993. She lives in Willow, Alaska, with her husband Mike.